Your Personal Power-Up

FIVE STEPS TO TAKE CONTROL OF YOUR LIFE AND CAREER

BRENDA MCGLOWAN-FELLOWS, Ph.D.
and
CLAUDEWELL S. THOMAS, M.D., M.PH.

Copyright © 2010 Brenda McGlowan-Fellows, Ph.D. and Claudewell S. Thomas, M.D., M.PH.

All rights reserved. No portion of this book may be reproduced, stored in a retrieval system, or transmitted in any form or by any means—electronic, mechanical, photocopy, recording, scanning, or other—except for brief quotations in critical reviews or articles, without the prior written permission of the publisher.

Published in Salt Lake City, Utah by Leadership Excellence.

Leadership Excellence titles may be purchased in bulk for educational, business, fund-raising, or sales promotional use. For information, please e-mail kens@eep.com.

All case studies, anecdotes, and other narratives are composite stories taken from a variety of actual case histories. Names and details have been changed.

Library of Congress Cataloging-in-Publication Data

ISBN: 978-1-930771-37-6

Printed in the United States of America

Advance Praise

"This is a masterpiece whose time has come! The clear and beautiful simplicity in this articulation of the evolving continuum of the complexity of understanding and growing one's life within the context of personal and professional development in the work environment is masterful. Written from the inside out, through an integration of mind, heart, and spirit from her own personal evolution, Dr. Fellows has outlined a process of universal truth in very specific and particular steps that speak to the souls of all of us who seek to hold and enhance not only our personal selves but also our professional personas in life. This culmination of research and soul search has brought together a reflected wisdom that transcends books written merely from the mind as mere syntheses of theories and pop psychologies. This book of transformation will accomplish what libraries of other books have failed to provide: a clear path to personal understanding and professional courage."

Dr. Roger Desmarais, Ph.D., President,
Corporate Systemics Inc. (CSI)
Consultant and Professor

"Magnificent! I enjoyed taking those five powerful steps."

Kathryn D. Peoples, MSCC, Chair
American Heart Association, Auction Committee
President, Peoples & Associates Consulting, LLC

"*Your Personal Power-Up* speaks a universal truth"

Angela McGlowan,
Bestselling Author, *Bamboozled*
Political Strategist & Former Congressional Candidate
President, Political Strategies & Insights, Inc.

"I wish I had access to this book when struggling to make early professional career decisions. Identifying the inner reference group and their insistent messages is clearly a step necessary for maintaining an uncompromising source of inner energy and focus. This book while based on award winning research is replete with actual life situations which clearly illustrate the point of the research based conclusions."

Dr. Donald M. Ehat, Ed.D.
Consultant, Manager, Professor, Continuing Student of Life.

"This book is very timely for those engaged in a management education program or a voluntary (or involuntary) career transition. Contemporary academic programs need to challenge students to "Power-Up" in the words of the authors in order to compete in the global marketplace. Current Economic conditions are leading to career disruption for so many unsuspecting professionals. We all need to arm ourselves with the best the literature has to offer regarding personal development. Toward this end, I found the discussions of handling negative self, the need for mentoring and the opportunities of multiculturalism to be particularly relevant. Too often we academics teach from anecdotal information. Dr. Fellows has provided valuable insights based on solid research as well as extensive field experience. The five steps outlined in the book represent a practical guide to personal and professional enhancement of mind, body and (dare I say) soul. I have added this book to my recommended reading list for my students and professional colleagues alike."

Dr. Eugene Muscat, Ed.D., Founding Director
USF Executive MBA Program
University of San Francisco,
School of Business and Professional Studies

"This book moves beyond the typical "self-help" genre by tapping original research conducted by Dr. Fellows and presented in a deep and detailed way. As you read, you will find that these authors encourage, explain and give you the necessary tools to tap your positive side; to boost your personal "power up."

Dr. Aaron D. Anderson, Ph.D., author of forthcoming book,
Engaging Resistance:How Ordinary People Successfully Champion Change

"A practical guide to help you get 'unstuck' from a job that may be the wrong fit for you. This book gives you an easy step by step pathway and useful tools so that you can have a more enjoyable work experience even given today's tough job environment."

Dr. B. Lynn Ware, Ph.D., President, Integral Talent Systems, Inc.

"The need for self knowledge is as old as mankind and we have been alerted to this at least 3,000 years ago by Isaiah, followed by Socrates who advised us that, 'The unexamined life is not worth living'.

"This volume provides fresh perspectives on how to navigate complex social environments, while minimizing the negative impact of the trauma, all too often accompanying the early socialization process. This book serves as a primer on how to contend with the ghosts of one's past and transform them into sources of positive instruments while negotiating a myriad of everyday challenges.

" 'When to cooperate and when to compete,' is a core issue that may never be addressed appropriately. Failure to confront it, is to guarantee an ever present darkness, which we, as humans are capable of illuminating. Classical works bear reinterpretation in every age and the examples provided in this book add to its contemporaneous value for our time. There is much to be learned from this volume and most importantly, where it may fail to provide concrete answers, it at least forces the reader to think. And we all know how difficult thinking can be."

Dr. Jacob Jay Lindenthal, Ph.D., Dr.PH.
Professor, Department of Psychiatry
Director: Institute for the Public Understanding of Health and Medicine
University of Medicine and Dentistry—New Jersey Medical School

We cannot avoid using the personal pronoun "I" constantly. Despite this the concept of "the self" to which it refers has always been and remains a contentious issue. Gilbert Ryle has famously dismissed it as "the ghost in the machine." Fellows and Thomas do not pretend to solve all the dilemma's the concept of "self" represents, but they do bring the "ghost" out of the shadows so that we can see it and give it substance in its most essential context: the inescapable everyday workplace. More than theory or philosophy, their book is a guide to helping the "self" empower itself on the grounds of reason and compassionate understanding. Best of all, it fulfills the edict that where it clarifies, it heals.

Bernard J. Bergen, Ph.D.
Professor Emeritus of Sociology and Psychiatry
Dartmouth Medical School and Dartmouth College

"Most of us are unhappy in our work situation. Many of us dread going to work. The lessons start with self-understanding and then converge on the need to exercise personal control over proximal events in the work situation to enhance feelings of empowerment. To be beneficial, the book's lessons should be considered in relation to compelling objective factors rooted in the work situation, how such factors impinge on the person and whether they are within the person's range of control."

Dr. Lloyd H. Rogler, Ph.D.
Albert Schweitzer Professor in the Humanities, Emeritus
Fordham University

Dedication

This book is dedicated to my parents, Professor James and Alberta McGlowan, and my husband, Cedric, in honor of your continued, unyielding love and support.

Contents

Foreword 15
Introduction: *Getting Unstuck* 17
  Lack of Satisfying Working Relationships With Others
  False Assumptions and Stereotyping
  Gender Discrimination
  Big Brother Syndrome
  Global Competition
  Fear of Change and the Future
  Inability to Keep Pace With Change
  Don't Worry, We're not Going to Label You

Part I 30
Chapter 1: Who Are You? (Step One: Know Yourself) 30
  It's a Self-Identity Issue: You Need to Know Who You Are
  Look Yourself in the Eye
  Beware, You May Have to Get Emotional!
  Where's Your Heart?
  What Does It All Add Up To?
  Find the Pain
  Feeling a Little Stressed?
  Face the Mirror
  Dig Up Your Past: Discovering the Archaeology of Your Identity
  Family History: Swinging on the Branches of Your Family Tree
  Sandbox Memories: Digging for Answers
  Are You Captive of Family Expectations?
  Getting Past Your Past

Chapter 2: What's in Your Label Box?
(Step Two: Resolve Contradictions) 51
  Look at Your Labels: Your Expectations Versus Everyone Else's
  Open Your Box of Labels: Are They Useful or Harmful?
  Classify Your Labels: From Home to Your Five o'Clock Shadow
  Check Your Labels at the Door: Did Your Roles and Labels Ever Fit?
  Clash of the Titans: Life Versus Work
  Breaking Free and Breaking Through the Looking Glass
  If the Label Doesn't Fit, Dump It

Chapter 3: Taking the Risk (Step Three: Embrace Change; Enable Yourself and Others) 68
    The Two Forces Within: Know Which One to Use
    Are You Keeping Up the Status Quo?
    Take the Risk and Leave Your Mummy
    Breaking Free of the Fear
    Harnessing the Wind and Striving Full Speed
    How's the Weather? Avoiding the Weather Vane
    Ethically Speaking
    They're Alive in You
    Beyond the Status Quo: The Proof of the Pudding

Chapter 4: Rounding Up the Allies (Step Four: Get Comfortable) 83
    Identifying and Preserving the Possibility of Change
    Understanding the Corporate Culture and Your Frame of Reference
    The Where, What, Why
    The Who, and the How
    Flexing Your Muscles: Finding Your Rightful Place
    Self-Efficacy
    Perseverance
    Intrapersonal Empowerment
    Interpersonal Skills
    Will the Leader Please Stand Up?
    Rounding Up Your Allies
    How Far Your Alliances Can Be Stretched: What Can You
        Count on From Others?
    What Can You Count on From Yourself?

Chapter 5: Satisfaction: Creating a Workplace Context (Step Five: Carpe Diem; Seize the Day) 102
    Analyzing and Understanding Your Existing Work Context
    The Risk Factor: Maintaining Your Work Context After You've
        Created It
    Essential Ethics: Being a Person of All Seasons Versus Situational
        Ethics
    Individuality in the Corporate World
    The Characteristics of a Strategic Leader
    Strategic Leaders and Teams
    Exemplary Strategic Leadership Practices
    Lead by Example
    Create, Encourage, and Inspire a Shared Vision
    Be an Appropriate Risk Taker
    Collaborator, Motivator, and Trust Builder
    Enable and Empower Others

Five Steps and Beyond

Part II 125
Chapter 6: Coaching, Mentoring and Psychotherapy 125
Outside Help
How Coaches Can Help
Will You Let Me Be Your Shadow? The Mentoring Paradigm
Mentors: The Career Makers
Are We All Going Crazy? The Psychotherapy Paradigm

Chapter 7: Avoiding the Downside of Success 135
Where the Rubber Meets the Road: What is Success?
The Celebrity Trap
Their Definitions or Yours: Should You Leave Your Roots Behind?
It Hurts So Badly: Sometimes Success and Failure Feel the Same
Stretched to Success
Leaving the Negative Self Behind
Personal Trolls, Personal Demons: Voices of the Negative Self
What is the Negative Self?
The Carrot or the Whip? Learning How to Choose Reward
    Over Punishment
You Recognize Them, Do They Recognize You? Revisiting Your Family
Getting Beyond the Negative Self

Chapter 8: Women: Getting Over the "Little Lady" Syndrome 159
Overcoming the Restricting Images of the Past
The Mentoring Dyad: Characteristics and Pitfalls
Is It an Issue of Gender, Age, or Race?
The Glass and Concrete Ceilings
Coping Strategies
Barriers to Women's Advancement
The Secrets of Successfully Mentoring Women
Are You on the Path to Power?

Chapter 9: Men: Winning Over the Warrior King 180
The Cult of the Warrior
On Mentoring Men
Does Gender Matter?
Men Mentoring Women
Lending a Helping Hand: Men and Women Working Together
Can We Talk? Communication Styles and Gender
Gender Wars: Bridging the Gap

Chapter 10: Embracing the Challenge of Change 193
   Tracking the Trends
   Multiculturalism: The Kaleidoscope of Opportunity
   Perceived and Perceiving
   Don't Lose Yourself
   Building the Cultural Bridge
   Bringing It All Together
   A Satisfying Sense of Success

End Notes 208
Acknowledgements 211
About the Authors 212

Foreword

Your Personal Power-Up is a revolutionary guide that enables you to peel back the layers and discover your true self. It will give you the tools to tap into your true potential, embrace change, and be comfortable in your own skin. It will help you identify factors that have shaped you, and resolve contradictions that influence your decisions. The result: a more confident and successful you, both in your career and in life.

A large amount of your life is spent at work, so we'll spend a lot of time on techniques that will help you succeed there. Success, in this case, translates into personal empowerment, an ability to enjoy work: to feel excited, committed, engaged, and passionate about it. Most importantly, success on the job—no matter what your income or status level—means you can perform the task and still be comfortable with *who you are*: no games, no workday masks, no pretending to be someone you're not. So many of us, especially business professionals and those employed by large corporations, often have to contend with challenges that make it tough to enjoy work. And that makes it tough to really succeed.

You may have to maneuver every day through a minefield of prickly personalities, demanding bosses, lethargic subordinates, discrimination, misinformation, underhandedness, and plain old-fashioned stupidity. A 2009 poll published in *Gallup Management Journal* showed that only 29 percent of American employees felt truly engaged and committed at work and had a passion for what they did.[1] Studies indicate that 98 percent of corporations could do more to make the workplace worker friendly. Of course, some businesses are more committed to workplace harmony than others, and a random sample of U.S. companies would reveal a range of office environments from hospitable to hostile. If you find yourself working in an organization toward the less agreeable side of that scale, your average day on the job is often stressful, frustrating, and unfulfilling—and sometimes it's miserable. Or maybe it isn't you but rather your spouse, friend, or another important person in your life who is trapped in a job where he or she is an underappreciated cog in a gigantic, relentlessly self-serving machine.

The good news is that it doesn't have to be that way. You possess the power to transform your workplace experience from something hollow and stress inducing into an opportunity you look forward to every morning. This book will explain how to do it, step by step. You can learn to cope successfully with almost anything the office throws at you and still be comfortable in your own skin. This isn't a book about making a new self; it's about discovering, celebrating, and empowering your true self, and then guiding that true you to contentment in your career.

Some of life's challenges, such as inner conflict, are partially derived from your family, early childhood experiences, spouses, partners, friends, workplace expectations, and society's labels to which you inappropriately respond—so we'll also learn to understand these as a way to find career success. Labels carried around as baggage are inappropriate in the workplace, inhibiting your ability to avoid missteps, and sabotaging—even derailing—your career through inappropriate risk taking. These labels don't empower you, they limit your ability to succeed. In the pages that follow, you'll see how to exchange these labels for interactive roles, which help you change your behavior as your situation changes. At home you may be a father or a mother, but at work you may be an executive, manager, or subordinate and must act accordingly.

Your Personal Power-Up—based on my (Dr. Brenda Fellows) award-winning 2003 empirical and focus group research and further corroborated by my 2007 research—enables you to realize success at work and in life by following five critical steps. Part I explains in detail how to utilize these five steps to move from feelings of stress and dissatisfaction to a state of confident control on the job. Part II highlights some of the most common roadblocks to implementing this process and how to get around them. A unique combination of real-life vignettes, case studies, thought-provoking sidebars, and exercises will help you take charge of your life, move forward with a purpose, and use Your Personal Power-Up to navigate change, control your emotions, and remove unseen obstacles.

We hope you will find the journey ahead helpful, and that *Your Personal Power-Up* will soon lead you to new heights of enjoyment and achievement in your career . . . and in life.

—*Dr. Brenda Fellows*
—*Dr. Claude Thomas*

Introduction: Getting Unstuck

Whether you think that you can, or that you can't, you are usually right.

—Henry Ford, American industrialist (1863–1947)

Are you stuck in your job?

Do you feel trapped at work between the fear of moving ahead and worry about falling behind? Are you increasingly anxious about what goes on at the office? Do you have a gnawing worry that you haven't mastered your job and you don't really know what's expected of you? Are you just trying to get by, hanging on by your fingernails?

You are not alone. In this day and age, due to advances in technology and growing global competition for jobs, many employees are feeling an increased level of anxiety. Regardless of position, power, or income, they feel the ground shifting and aren't confident or comfortable in making decisions, trusting their instincts, or exerting power over life changes and directions that should be their alone to control.

So if you feel stressed on the job, you've got plenty of company. My extensive research confirms that employees are genuinely anxious about their job security, prospects for promotion, and career success in general. Even the seemingly enviable and well-paid participants in my study—successful corporate middle managers and executives—reported feeling uncomfortable in their own skin, powerless, and stagnant. In a word, they felt stuck.

Through both empirical and qualitative research, I've identified unconscious attitudes that underlie the hiring, retention, and firing of business professionals functioning at the middle manager to senior executive level in corporate America.

My research showed that many people shared a generalized anxiety about employment, retention (that is, keeping the job once you've been hired), and, ultimately, success in the corporate realm. This anxiety was associated with memories from deep within, which evoked very strong emotions. Those emotions seemed to stem from early childhood, a time when most of us are socialized—trained in the norms and values of our families and culture.

The focus group aspect of my study sought to identify the specific source of this anxiety. Throughout the study, business professionals, including senior executives, voiced a sense of frustration and powerlessness at work, which was a recurrent theme that emerged. Many of the employees felt a lack of collegial support and acknowledgement, which, over time, caused them to question whether they were valued. Long-felt fears of isolation, abandonment, and being left out (which appeared to be lurking just beneath the surface) emerged, leaving them with profound feelings of discomfort and powerlessness.

The ability to collaborate within the organization, build healthy and productive work relationships, provide support and guidance, and to be mentored was often compromised as a result. Another critical skill—the ability to manage relationships with colleagues and understand when to cooperate and when to compete—was directly linked to the ability to succeed in increasingly complex corporate structures. In order to recognize how personal dynamics may be an impediment to fostering healthy relationships and competition at work, you must peel back the layers to self-identify, resolve core contradictions, accept and use change as a key advantage.

All participants in the research study, without exception, experienced this deep anxiety despite their promotions, advanced positions, and titles. Each participant held a professional position in corporate America, earned at least a six-figure income, and was considered successful by nearly all measures. Yet despite all of this, not one of the participants really felt comfortable in his or her own skin! This allowed a feeling of powerlessness and stagnation to set in.

Clearly shown were men's and women's differing perspectives with regard to their ability to be hired, retained, and promoted in corporate America. Seventy-five men and women leaders of all races between the ages of 21 to 65, who were mid-managers and senior level executives employed by global corporations, participated in the study. Participants were asked to explore questions critical to their life experiences. The combination of both quantitative and qualitative methods allowed for the most objective yet thorough understanding of factors facilitation hiring and promotion for men and women in the workplace.

Men and women perceived factors of both gender and race as impacting their work situations. Women reported less involvement with policy formulation, viewed themselves as having less decision-making authority, and in receipt of fewer available resources. They also viewed themselves as receiving less respect and "appropriate attention" from both superiors and peers, and felt they were impeded by a glass ceiling (impacting all women) or a concrete ceiling (specifically impacting women of color) in their organizations. Many women pointed to difficulties with being mentored and mentoring others (of the same and of a different gender or race) and believed that mentoring and having access to influential people was the most important factor contributing to being hired. Also, a lack of solidarity among coworkers and stereotyped gender roles and labels were viewed as major obstacles in the workplace.

Men and women viewed existence in corporate America differently. During focus group discussions women cited issues of gender as critical to the hiring and promotion process. Whether true or not, the experiences of these women suggested that hiring managers (mostly men) possessed negative perceptions of women. Conversely, men felt that their gender empowered them. More striking was the sense, from both women and men, that issues of gender impacted women's ability to be respected at all levels.

A significant finding emerged from a societal, psychological, and gender perspective. The research suggests that because males traditionally have been in power, their attitudes and perceptions have had a disproportionate effect on workplace behavior. The research implies that a lack of empathy in the workplace, and the resultant callousness that occurs on a daily basis, helps maintain others in a marginalized work experience. The resultant disparity within the organization reduces the potential for effective performance, resulting in a drop in productivity, loyalty, and employee retention.

For those of you who are struggling to move through the corporate ranks, wrestling with these issues of respect and power takes predominance over factors that are recognized by theorists, consultants, and executive coaches as the best strategies for advancement—such as mentoring, access to influential people, fitting in the corporate culture, and job performance. Thus, the challenges faced by corporate employees become a dichotomous one: choosing to acquiesce to the emotional rudiments of corporate life, (seeking status, recognition, and acceptance) or deciding (dangerously) to march to the beat of your unique and personal drummer.

A majority of the participants, both men and women, felt impacted by their inability to be accepted and upwardly mobile in the workplace, prompting them to rethink the concept of job security. There would appear to be no organizational experience or safe haven that clearly suggests corporate employees have arrived. The necessary markers lie in the recognition of who you are and the ability to create your own context, leading you to empowerment and allowing *purposive striving* in your career and life to define the path of success.

Purposive striving is an individual attribute that logically links to the effectiveness of your career. One potential aspect of that linkage is called *ethical profitability*. It means making a profit without destroying the competition and is dependent upon the quality of your product and the effectiveness of your workers to gain market share—rather than using measures that corner the market and destroy competition. Both concepts —ethical profitability and purposive striving—come from a *melioristic* framework, which is simply a belief that the betterment of mankind can be accomplished through man's efforts. The most important thing to remember, however, is the ability to purposively strive is a journey, not a destination.

In other words, once you know who you are deep down, you can confidently set a direction for your business career; you can strive with a specific, focused purpose with the objective of taking others along with you. There will be less wasted motion, fewer dead ends, and fewer unresolved contradictions. You'll stop spinning around like a weather vane, buffeted by the winds of change and overreacting to external forces.

Effective living, happiness at work and in your life, depends ultimately on your ability to learn, adapt, and grow. It isn't about money— though money is certainly a great incentive and there's nothing wrong with doing well financially—because there are an awful lot of miserable and stressed workers out there who are making millions. Success is measured internally as well as externally. Without the internal component, deep meaning, personal success, and the satisfying assurance of a job well and rightly done will elude you. Our purpose here is to help you gain control of yourself, your work environment, your career and your life; to help you become self empowered and realize success at work without relinquishing your individuality or getting crushed in the wheels of the corporate machine.

Tommy and Tina Telecommuter

You don't have to be a well-paid corporate manager to be stuck in a stressful job with no evident means of escape. Let's take a look at characters we'll call Tommy and Tina Telecommuter. When Tommy and Tina first started working from home, they thought it was the best idea they ever had. They set aside a comfortable, quiet area in the house exclusively for business, determined to enjoy the flexibility and efficiency of telecommuting without letting it interfere with their home lives. It wasn't long, though, before work started spilling over into their private time. Persistent office problems soon wormed their way into the family; they found themselves barking at their children, and at each other, because they were irritated or stressed about what was happening on the job.

Tommy and Tina's experience highlights a key source of trouble in the workplace today: it's all but impossible to separate home and work environments in the digital age. Wherever you are, you're always on call.

> DO YOU EVER FEEL STRESSED AT WORK? HOW DOES THIS IMPACT YOUR HEALTH AND YOUR HOME LIFE?

Do you feel a little stressed? It's not surprising, because your stress levels have increased due to workplace stress if you're between the ages of 45 and 54 according to a 2009 survey by the American Psychological Association. The culprit is not only work, but also money. Approximately three out of four of you—or 81 percent of men, and 68 percent of women —or slightly over half of you say work causes you great stress; this number has risen significantly since 2008. Men at 86 percent say money woes are like a thorn in your side. Men, at 88 percent and women, at 77 percent, between the ages of 35 to 44, cite experience stress over earning money as a main concern.[1] Workplace stress causes you to leave your job, look for another job, or even turn down a promotion due to stress in your place of employment. The study confirms what millions of workers feel intuitively: stress on the job spills over to become stress in your personal life; it can even make you physically sick. Now more than ever, you and your colleagues are trying to live in two different and usually incompatible worlds at once—the world of work and career, and the world of home and family and refuge. At home you can be yourself, but at work you have to be somebody else; you're forced to live a bicultural life. What's important is that you learn to manage your stress, and not let it manage you.

You don't have to look far to find other challenges and irritations in the workplace that jump out in high relief.

Lack of Satisfying Working Relationships with Others

My study revealed that employees feel a strong sense of isolation and disconnection in the workplace. They miss a sense of support from their colleagues and long for approval and acknowledgment. They're not sure when to collaborate and when to compete. They wonder if their contribution really counts and if what they do really matters. Their ambition and desire to succeed fades because they feel shackled by the system: what they think and desire seems meaningless and futile to their bosses. They want friends and mentors, but aren't sure how to cultivate those connections. Desperate for feedback, they never know if they've finally made it or are on the brink of being fired.

False Assumptions and Stereotyping

Workers feel trapped by first impressions of themselves. A woman applying for a job or working in a department full of men may feel like her colleagues see her first as a woman and not as a professional: she's weak and "too feminine." People of color who work in a predominately Caucasian office environment may sense they're treated differently because of assumptions about their race or heritage. A promising new employee with an ethnic or unusual name may be unfairly branded with certain stereotypes before he has an opportunity to demonstrate who he really is and what he can do. An older worker may not be able to impress a younger boss, no matter how good his performance is; conversely, a young executive might have a hard time convincing an older staff that he has what it takes to be in charge. The fact that the workforce is getting steadily younger and more culturally diverse makes this issue all the more important. According to the U.S. Census Bureau, there are 79.8 million American workers under age thirty, already outnumbering the 78.5 million baby boomers still on the job; and by 2050, the national working population will be more than 50 percent non-Caucasian.

Gender Discrimination

Though discrimination has been officially against the law for decades, it is far from gone in the workplace. Women in my study reported being less involved in policy decisions and receiving less respect than their male counterparts. They said they had less access to mentors and less power than comparable men. Caucasian women spoke of a glass ceiling, a barrier to corporate advancement because of their gender, while women of color (meaning all non-Caucasian women) encountered a concrete ceiling, meaning an even more extreme bias against them. Men of color, workers with disabilities, older workers, and others often have to contend with an undercurrent of discrimination that hampers advancement and enhances stress.

Big Brother Syndrome

A 2005 Electronic Monitoring and Surveillance survey from the American Management Association and the ePolicy Institute reported that three-fourths of organizations surveyed admitted to having some form of employee surveillance, a 27 percent increase over 2001.[2] Many companies monitor e-mail messages, track Internet usage, employ video surveillance, record telephone conversations, and review voice mail messages. The U.S. Bureau of Labor Statistics reports that three-fourths of the private sector's eighty million workers are employed "at will," meaning they can be fired for almost any reason, even for no reason at all. According to the American Civil Liberties Union, two million at-will employees are fired annually.

Global Competition

The Brookings Institution (in findings echoed by the Society of Human Resource Management, American Management Association, American Psychological Association, and Society of Industrial/Organizational Psychology) reports that by 2015, U.S. businesses will lose an estimated 3.3 million service jobs to offshoring, the practice of replacing American employees with cheaper workers overseas. This trend intensifies the pressure on organizations to hold down salaries and benefits in order to compete in the global economy—even though a generation ago CEOs made an average of forty times their workers' salary, while today's counterpart earns four hundred times as much. For many workers, health-care coverage, retirement programs, family leave, flexible hours, and other desirable benefits are often being reduced or eliminated. Employees may find themselves working longer hours for less pay, taking a second job, subject to more fierce workplace competition, working involuntarily beyond their expected retirement dates, being retrained for lower paying jobs, or simply laid off. People feel pressured to push themselves harder than ever, curtailing vacations and keeping their BlackBerrys within reach day and night. The average American employee works more than forty-eight hours a week, according to a 2006 report from the International Labor Organization, which defined it as "excessive."

A 2006 Metro Economies report argues that there is a "surge in the economy, but with lower paying jobs."[3] Jobs lost in the last three years paid $43,000 annually; jobs created in the next two years will pay an average of $36,000 annually.

Many organizations' mission statements articulate equality in the hiring and promotion of all employees as a goal or standard. But the gap in gender-based wages is widening. Women comprise half of the corporate leadership positions (managers and professional specialists). In Fortune 500 companies, only 6.7 percent were top earners, 15.4 percent were officers holding board seats, and 3 percent of board directors were women of color (as suggested in a 2007 Catalyst report on corporate leadership), clearly indicating gender and race disparity. Women are leaving corporate America at a rate of 420 per day, twice the rate of men; while many women climb the corporate ladder, others leave to gain control over their lives, follow their passion, and have work/life balance.[4]

A 2009 Catalyst report on women and diversity demonstrates that women comprised 467 percent of the work force and hold 51.4 percent of professional, managerial, and related positions.⁵

Fear of Change and the Future

According to the U.S. Census Bureau, there are 79.8 million workers under the age of thirty who are Gen Yers (also called millennials), and they're working side by side with 78.5 million Gen Xers and baby boomers).⁶ Many baby boomers are being replaced by Gen Yers, who are now "the boss," causing anxiety for those who have worked many years to now answer to someone their child's age, someone still "wet behind the ears."

Fearing job loss, people tend to keep their heads down and hold on, hoping for the best yet resigned to the assumption that there's nothing they can do to improve their situation. They dread the imagined consequences of challenging the status quo. Though they dream of fulfilling, enjoyable work, they can't imagine changing their corporate culture to conform to their personal desires, nor finding happiness in their current positions. They endure the unending conflict and the tension of being one person at work and another at home.

Job changes, advancements in technology and communications, the ever-increasing influence of the media, and the blurring boundary between work and personal life are among a number of changes that cause conflict. It's easy to get caught up in this dictated life flux and lose sight of what's most important: who you are.

Furthermore, the negative effect of this inner conflict is showing. A 2006 Gallup *Management Journal* survey showed differing perspectives among U.S. job satisfaction: 27 percent of American workers are engaged (or have a connection) with their organization and passion for their work. Over 70 percent of all Americans are either not engaged, unhappy with their jobs, or actively disengaged from their jobs. What does this suggest? Almost three of every four Americans have either lost any true loyalty to their company or job, or they've mentally given up the fight, thrown in the towel, and have checked out altogether.⁷

American workers feel disconnected at work and they're losing the desire, push, and ambition to succeed because they don't see autonomy and ambition as effective in combating externally dictated movement or the lack of it. While human resource managers, training managers, and business leaders routinely prescribe more and better worker evaluations, raises, promotions, motivational conferences and training sessions, the problems go deeper than do the solutions.

HOW DO YOU FEEL ABOUT YOUR JOB? DO YOU LOVE IT OR TOLERATE IT BECAUSE YOU FEEL THAT YOU MUST? IS YOUR JOB SIMPLY A MEANS TO AN END OR DO YOU FIND IT TO BE QUITE FULFILLING?

Inability to Keep Pace with Change

Senior executives and managers implicitly understand that employees are the engine that drives business. Yet despite the indispensability of their employees, many organizations don't know how to develop individual potential even when they do hire the right people. The result is that the workplace does not maximize the potential for sustained superior performance.

The rapid pace of change and the pervasiveness of technology create gaps between information and knowledge, and the task of transforming disparate pieces of information into cohesive and profitable knowledge has become a primary source of workplace anxiety. While technology might be the most dramatic example of change, it is external change, and there are important internal changes that often go unnoticed or unobserved. Despite the fact that you view yourself as stable over time, you are nonetheless involved in a lifelong process of change and adaptation. How often do you recognize internal change when you're in the midst of it? The answer is *not very often*.

Typically, you only recognize internal change during periods of major upheaval in your life. That's because in such periods, your very survival requires internal transitions that are obvious and are generally characterized by feelings of anxiety, unease, and a feeling that events have, indeed, changed you.

It doesn't matter what kind of change you undergo; "good" or "bad" changes both produce stress. While job loss or a family death are hard to miss, other life changes like marriage, a new baby, or a job promotion (all presumably joyous events) create similar levels of stress and produce anxiety.

It would appear that one third of the population embraces change and challenge, one third is opposed to change and challenge, and one third is willing to entertain the idea of change if the perceived risks involved are not too great and they can be assured that failure is not part of the risk. Risk is a part of the process that propels you onward and upward and places you ahead of the pack. The inevitability of change in the workplace and in your life need not be feared, but celebrated. It allows you to look at yourself with a greater understanding of the possibilities of who you are and can become. The truth is, change is constant and your ability to properly manage it is critical to your personal and professional success.

It has never been more important to be able to answer the question, "So who am I really?" Can you answer this question with conviction? It may not be as easy as it sounds. And if you're unable to answer, what does this suggest to you?

Unfortunately, many of you routinely ignore the importance of understanding who you truly are. You go about life without putting forth the effort to connect with who you are or spend adequate time engaging in some simple but necessary introspection. Thus you lack the ability to make the right decisions that will effectively lead you to move forward and progress in your career and life.

It is no surprise that you sometimes feel paralyzed and find yourself unable to act when the world around you demands action. A lack of trust may be a part of the problem. Many people, regardless of level or pay status, struggle to trust the world around them, especially at work. Nevertheless, they feel uncomfortable and distrustful of the corporate structure, their place in it, and its ability to reciprocate their trust.

To make matters worse, the separation between work and personal life is narrowing. Your failure to resolve personal and interpersonal problems spills over into the workaday world. Every day you carry the weight of family issues that have either never been clearly identified or completely resolved, and it increases the anxiety that inhibits you in your career and life.

A quick look at the history of the past 150 years tells us that every generation has felt it was living in an age of anxiety. Every era has had its financial crises and social upheavals and foreboding predictions about the future. But no other period has brought change at so fast a pace and made it so hard just to hold onto our individual personalities—the very *core self* each of us has deep inside that steers our lives and our thinking like a compass steers a ship. We live in the middle of the biggest storm of change in human history. So what do we do? What in the world can prevail against such a daunting list of obstacles?

Your Personal Power-Up, that's what!

DO YOU LOOK FORWARD TO CHANGE AND ACTIVELY EMBRACE IT, OR DO YOU FEAR IT?

Don't Worry, We're Not Going to Label You

There are numerous books that label or identify you as one type of personality or another. Personality types come in all different shapes and sizes, and are related to theories of personality structure. We do not subscribe to any personality theory and to us it is irrelevant whether you're one personality type or another. Remember, *Your Personal Power-Up* is about getting past roles and labels and moving beyond complacency or a status quo mind-set towards a fulfilling and rewarding career and life.

The chapters that follow contain the tools and information you need to turn your work experience from an unavoidable drudgery to a challenge that you look forward to with confidence every day. They will help you take control of both the internal and external processes that shape you. It all begins with discovering and celebrating who you really are, and ends with identifying and establishing the satisfying and personally enriching workplace environment you've always wanted. This can be accomplished in five steps.

Step One—Know Yourself: Identify who you are, and who people think you are. Begin aligning yourself with who you want to be (your *authentic self*). This means changing your behavior to accord with this discovery.

To reach your full workplace and career potential for satisfaction and success, you first have to understand who you are by peeling back the various layers of public persona that have formed over the years to get to your basic core. Your family and childhood, friends, relatives, and coworkers have all played a part in shaping you. Chances are you'll discover remarkable and encouraging characteristics along the way. A fresh sense of self-knowledge will encourage you to look ahead with new confidence and purpose, and will likely inspire you to change your behavior in order to conform to that new person you see in the mirror. You can then begin aligning yourself with the person you want to be.

Step Two—Resolve Contradictions: Identify who you are, who people think you are, and resolve the contradictions. Identify your roles and labels. Try to resolve the contradictions between who you believe yourself to be and who people think you are (this process leads to an identification and alignment of your authentic self).

The business world tends to make assumptions about you, stereotype you, throw labels at you, and generally gets it all wrong when it comes to understanding who you are and what you can do. Once you've discovered your "comfortable self," it's time to introduce everybody else to it by clearing away the old misconceptions and misinformation, jettisoning the emotional baggage other people have piled on you, and redefining yourself on your terms instead of theirs. Identify all those false and stress-inducing labels, then resolve the contradictions between who you *know* you are and who the world *thinks* you are. Align others with your newfound identity.

Step Three—Embrace Change; Enable Yourself and Others: Do not stand opposed to change. Accept change by learning to take risks appropriately. Work to understand differing cultural contributions, and accept them through facilitating working with diversity. Paradoxically, this facilitates self-understanding.

Change is coming and there's no way to stop it or get out of the way. Change is either your friend or your enemy; it will either swamp you or carry you forward into the future on top of a powerful wave of opportunity and fulfillment. Rather than making a futile—and very stressful—effort to stand against change, learn to accept change and make it work for you. The business world will continue to become more complex, more competitive, more diverse, and more demanding, and the successful worker will change and adapt along with it, discarding old expectations and limitations as he goes. Change brings risks, and learning to take appropriate risks—being neither reckless nor reclusive—is an important component of career success and satisfaction.

Step Four—Get Comfortable: Identify a context in which you can "strive" (even if it's theoretical), and find your rightful place in your organization.

Round up strategic allies, resolve personal conflicts with coworkers, identify political sensitivities, understand both the written and unwritten rules of your business, know when to collaborate and when to compete, enable and empower others, and sweep away the roadblocks that have prevented you from thriving on the job. Move from a place of conflict to one of cooperation, from what may be a sense of paralyzing stress to a refreshing sense of optimism and confidence.

Step Five—Carpe Diem: Seize the day and take control of your life by creating and claiming a workplace environment where you can succeed.

Now, how can you accomplish these five steps? First you use the way you feel to locate discomforting thoughts or ideas. Second, you think about the linkages and associations involved in those ideas. Third, you analyze and act to alter accompanying behavior.

In the chapters that follow, we'll break each of these steps down into a set of recommendations that flow logically from one to the next. They may not all be easy for you to do—different people will have strengths in different areas—but we hope they'll be easy to understand. The overarching goals are for you to get to know who you are, stop trying to be somebody you're not, learn to be comfortable in your own skin, and use that knowledge to move forward with purposive striving.

Are you a purposive striver in both your career and personal life? If not, how would you describe yourself?

While the situations you encounter may be outside your realm of control, the way you confront them and overcome them is not. Reading *Your Personal Power-Up* can give you the confidence to meet the challenges that you face and help you make appropriate decisions.

It all starts with an understanding of who you are.

Action Item
- Continue to read this book to take five powerful steps forward.

Part I

Chapter 1: Who Are You?

When you come to a fork in the road, take it.

—Yogi Berra, Major League Baseball player and manager (b. 1925)

Step One: Know Yourself
IDENTIFY WHO YOU ARE AND WHO PEOPLE THINK YOU ARE. BEGIN ALIGNING YOURSELF WITH WHO YOU WANT TO BE (YOUR AUTHENTIC SELF). THIS MEANS CHANGING YOUR BEHAVIOR ACCORDINGLY.

It's easy to lose sight of who you are. The world is constantly changing, and even when the change appears to be the same to a number of persons, the impact certainly varies. Cross-checking with other people, then, can become laborious and confusing.

Consider this parable: a man and woman were sitting in a room with two doors. One door had a sign that read, *Do not exit*. The other read, *Do not enter*. They both sat with their heads in their hands, not knowing which way to go. Each asked the other what to do, but they could not come up with an answer that satisfied them both. So they continued to sit and wait on the right answer that never came.

There's a classic scene in Lewis Carroll's *Alice in Wonderland* that depicts the dilemma of "becoming." When Alice comes to a difficult crossroads, she asks the Cheshire Cat, "Which way should I go?" His response is, "Where do you want to go? If you don't know where you want to go, it doesn't matter which direction you go in." And so it is with your own life. With each change in life, you come to a crossroads—a crossroads and a decision point. Take the workplace, for example. The crossroads you come to may range from a job change, new management, a promotion or layoff, to the rigors of day-to-day coping. Changes may go beyond the personal realm to include an evolving workforce and a global dynamic such as outsourcing. Even in your own home, you may begin to feel like a stranger because these shifts have created a society that is quite different from the homogeneity in which you have lived, and from which perspective you have viewed yourself in the past, whether accurately or not.

The only way you can know where you want to go when you come to a fork in the road is to know and be comfortable with who you are and what you can become. You can't move forward effectively and sustainably in life unless you know who you are. In the 1939 film *The Wizard of Oz*, Dorothy and her friends ask the wizard for specific things to help them move forward in life. The sad Tin Man asks for a heart, the posturing Cowardly Lion asks for courage, and the academically challenged Scarecrow asks for a brain. Misunderstood and regretful, Dorothy asks only to go home. Ultimately, what they all discover is that they don't need the wizard's help after all. They had the answers. They could have met their own needs all along because they themselves possessed the power and the desire to move forward. They just didn't know how to do it until they became fully aware of themselves. They needed some simple yet necessary introspection along with the ability to embrace change and take appropriate risks, which as they learned is easier said than done.

It's a Self-Identity Issue: You Need to Know Who You Are

It's easy to blame your anxiety on forces outside your control, but that doesn't help you come out on the winning side of change. No, you must look within. In order to adapt to change, you must know yourself well enough to be able to put yourself in the context of the changes around you. It starts with understanding who you are and where you come from. Without an adequate understanding of yourself, you cannot effectively move ahead in your career and life.

By examining and experimenting with your strengths and weaknesses, you remove your own self-imposed limits and make the inevitable need for personal change less onerous. This allows you to become confident in your decision making and empowered in your performance—in both your career and personal life.

When you gain a stronger understanding of who you are, you know what is basic to your core identity and what skills can enable you to bring forth your best efforts. You find relief from your feelings of discomfort as you recognize and remove subliminal personal obstacles, enabling you to tap into your true potential, reshape your personal and work environments (to the extent possible), and reduce the ability of outside influences to dictate what should or should not be important to you.

> DO YOU FEEL CONFLICT, ANXIETY, AND DISCOMFORT FROM EVENTS THAT HAPPEN AROUND YOU? DO YOU IGNORE THESE FEELINGS OR DO YOU TAKE ACTION?

If you don't know who you are, you're not going to know what to do with yourself. A nagging sense of conflict, anxiety, stress, and discomfort about everyday events tends to come around more and more often. You keep adding to your to-do list until the stack has grown so high it's a fire hazard. You don't know which direction to step off in. That means it's time to discover who you are and resolve the contradictions between the true, original, inner you and the person you've become on the outside. You can't move forward until you do.

Imagine you're driving down the road one day and your car's check-engine light comes on. It goes off right away, so you ignore it. For a few days afterward the light keeps coming on, warning you that something's wrong under the hood, but then it goes right off, so you keep on ignoring it. Finally one day the light comes on and stays on, the car stalls, and you're stranded in the middle of nowhere. Your car warned you several times to pay attention, but you ignored it and now have to suffer the consequences.

That light represents the inner you. Continuing to ignore it is going to strand you sooner or later. Knowing who you are will help you set your life to a rhythm of purpose and keep you moving smoothly ahead in the right direction.

You cannot fully embrace change or experience sustained success in your career and personal life until you know your comfortable (or basic) self—that *original* you, with all its characteristics and abilities. Once you know who that person is, you'll never be asking, "Which way should I go?" like Alice, or longing for something you already have like Dorothy and her friends. Understanding your comfortable (or basic) self eventually assures you that you can move ahead to new opportunities and successes in your career and in life, and shows you which direction to head. Without this understanding, you likely will face a future fearful of change and full of stagnant frustration.

When you're first learning to drive a car, you tend to drive where you're focusing. The same thing happens in life: you end up wherever you've been looking. You can complain about what life has become, but in general you live the life you've elected because of where you've put your focus. Your actions, decisions, and priorities should all revolve around what you actually *want* deep inside. If they don't—if your focus is not on the true desires that come out of your authentic self—you may bemoan the results, but your own misplaced priorities have led you to them.

So who are you really? While we can't reduce the answer to such an important question to a set of simple steps, there are three basic elements or phases in aligning yourself with who you truly are. It all begins by stepping back, taking a good look at yourself in the mirror and asking simple questions, such as "Who am I?" "Do I recognize myself?" and "Do I know my roots?" Going through the characteristics and features that define yourself isn't always easy. Some of them are impressive and desirable, while others are a little hard to admit. Until you tap into the deep inner feelings that reveal those components of who you are, you won't know yourself.

Look Yourself in the Eye

Take a good look. Looking at yourself in your car's rearview mirror is not good enough. In the response to the *Who am I?* question, more often than not you may identify outwardly visible characteristics. So, the story might go, "I'm a thirty-four-year-old Caucasian male from New York." Often there is a jump to professional titles or words that describe your work, such as, "I'm an investment banker," "I'm a senior production executive," or "I'm a senior engineer."

What you see first are the things you *want* to see first. Whether you realize it or not, the first things that come to mind are the ones you put the most importance on, for better or for worse.

WHAT ARE THE FIRST IMPRESSIONS YOU GET ABOUT YOURSELF WHEN YOU LOOK IN THE MIRROR?

They're the priorities you place on who you are, or at least who you think you are as you seek your basic or comfortable self; otherwise known as your authentic self. And they reveal quite a bit about you.

Sometimes your relationships with others come out first: husband, wife, father, mother, daughter, brother, sister, grandparent, or aunt. Your social, religious, and political affiliations occupy some of your definition: Democrat, Republican, environmentalist, Hindu, Protestant, agnostic, or Christian Scientist are some that come to mind. Your origins and heritage occupy yet other space: Asian, American Indian, Black, Caucasian, Indian, Latino, Pacific Islander, Midwesterner, Southerner, a Smith or a Winthrop. Sometimes the definition includes activities that you love: gourmet chef, gardener, and animal lover. You are a complicated blend of many things.

If you're having a hard time getting past outward representations of yourself, such as your race, gender, or physical features, then try this exercise in a comfortable place. Create a comfortable environment and relax. It may even help to think of things you find relaxing: a walk on the beach, enjoying a cup of coffee in a nice café, a glass of wine on a city terrace, listening to your favorite classical music, or traveling to an exciting vacation spot.

Beware, You May Have to Get Emotional!

Peeling back the layers and discovering who you are is an emotional thing. Discovering who you are, identifying conflicts within yourself, and changing for the better are all emotional pursuits. This can be an intense process and it's not for sissies. It will require some real soul-searching and introspection, using an innate capability known as *emotional intelligence*.

Your emotional intelligence is a measure of your deeper processing skills, more than just on a superficial level. It includes skills such as the ability to observe, introspect, identify, shape thinking, and harness emotions. You can measure your emotional intelligence by identifying your capacity to adapt to the people and environment around you without loss of self-identity (your sense of self).

ARE YOU EMOTIONALLY INTELLIGENT?

It significantly influences your ability to understand yourself and confidently face the changes and stressful situations of your life. It includes your sensitivity to others, your flexibility, and your ability to go beyond the obvious. It's about engaging the whole process of self-identification in the context of your life.

In order to get out of your discomfort zone and utilize your emotional intelligence (at least in principle), you must:

1. Challenge your preconceived notions
2. Cultivate your ability to empathize
3. Be flexible and willing to change what isn't working

The better developed your emotional intelligence, the more easily you will be able to see and accept aspects of yourself and others that you may not like or agree with. Being honest with yourself is not an altogether comfortable experience. It requires a willingness to face your fears and openly recognize that you may be in situations where you're uncomfortable.

Learning to strive—to identify the right goal for you based on who you are and head resolutely toward it while being inclusive of others—is an emotional experience. Change is engaged at the emotional level first, where emotions act collectively as an intensifying catalyst that makes the experience more intense and profound. At that level it's either embraced or stymied, and action or inaction then follows. The resulting action (or inaction) is a secondary process. Your emotions act collectively as a catalyst that makes the experience of change more intense and profound.

The experience of change is not a process of serenity, but to the degree you positively connect emotion to the creative process of change, you will not only find increased success in your life, but respite from the inner turmoil and distress that your complacency and resistance to change is trying to avoid. Don't fear the inevitability of change—embrace and celebrate it. It allows you to look at yourself in the mirror with a greater understanding of who you are and who you can become.

In your journey to become all that you can be, the key is how well you develop and utilize your own emotional intelligence. The development of your ability to observe, introspect, identify, adapt your thinking, harness your emotions accordingly is essential, leading to self mastery and control; these, in turn, leading to increased personal growth, productivity, and empowerment.

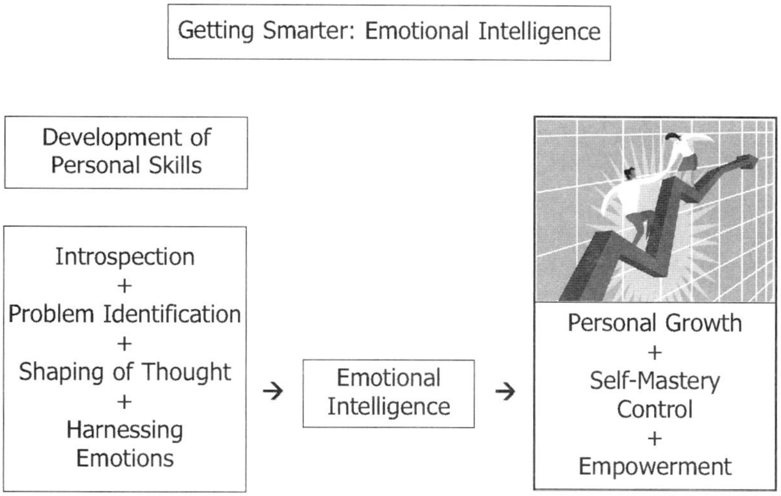

Getting Smarter: Emotional Intelligence

Development of Personal Skills

Introspection
+
Problem Identification
+
Shaping of Thought
+
Harnessing Emotions

→ Emotional Intelligence →

Personal Growth
+
Self-Mastery Control
+
Empowerment

Diagram 1.1

Diagram 1.1 illustrates the factors that go into the development of that personal skill called emotional intelligence. The right side of the diagram illustrates the result of successful application of emotional intelligence. Notice how both climbers show benefit.

To the degree that you have developed your own emotional intelligence, you will be able to look at yourself in the mirror and see who you truly are. When was the last time you looked yourself in the eye?

ONCE YOU HAVE GOTTEN PAST THE OUTWARD APPEARANCES THAT YOU BELIEVE DEFINE YOU (I.E., ASIAN, CAUCASIAN, BLACK, INDIAN, LATINO, PRETTY, OVERWEIGHT, SKINNY, ATHLETIC, TALL, AND SO ON), TAKE A DEEP BREATH, CREATE THAT RELAXING ATMOSPHERE, AND ASK YOURSELF AGAIN, "WHAT DO I SEE WHEN I SEE ME?"

Where's Your Heart?

If you're learning to drive, the tendency is to drive to where you are focusing. If you apply that to life, you end up where you have been looking. Sure, you hear a lot of complaining about what life has become, but in general you live the life you've elected because of where you've put your focus. Your actions, decisions, and even the priorities you've placed on things all should revolve around what you actually *want*, deep inside. You may bemoan the consequences of those actions, but it's your priorities that have led you to *be* who you are today.

Similarly, when it comes to knowing who you are, the things you see first are the things you *want* to see first. Whether you realize it or not, the first things that come to mind—especially the ones that are hard to admit—are always the ones you put the most importance on, for good and for bad. They're the priorities you place on who you are, or at least who you think you are. And they reveal quite a bit about who you are.

Some of you put the negatives out first, and save the positive points of who you are for last, as if admitting your faults is prerequisite to being admitted to the praise-your-positives party. Perhaps others of you are all too eager when it comes to bringing out the best in yourself, saving no room for the negatives or the dark side.

WHAT ATTRIBUTES ARE MOST IMPORTANT TO YOU? HOW DOES YOUR PROFESSIONAL TITLE OR POSITION PLAY INTO THE MIX? IS IT THE "SOCIAL" YOU THAT IS MOST IMPORTANT OR IS IT THAT YOU ARE THE ONE WHO GETS HIS OR HER WORK DONE?

What Does It All Add Up To?

Inevitably, going through the list of characteristics and features that you believe make up *you* isn't always easy. Chances are, some of the parts that make up who you are may be a little hard to admit, while others you may freely endorse.

Until you determine what feelings you have deep inside with regard to the characteristics, traits, and titles that you identified as being you, you don't know yourself. Have you had the experience of feeling more comfortable with or trusting somebody better when they've given you some cues about how they feel about a particular issue or task? You will also be more comfortable with yourself when you've done this exercise, as difficult as it may be.

Find the Pain

It's natural to run from pain and flock to fun. We gravitate toward pleasing feelings and experiences and try to avoid suffering and hardship at all costs. The irony is that you can learn as much from pain as you can from pleasure. Certainly you are going to learn different things.

Pain can be a major motivation. Take, for example, the phrases, "If you had a gun to your head . . ." or "If your life depended on it . . ." You rarely hear anyone say, "If your trip to Disneyland depended on it . . ." At first blush, pain would appear to provoke more decisive action than pleasure (unless the pleasure stake is very high). You can learn a great deal from hard lessons, things that the easy road never teaches. But who wants pain? You try to snuff out pain by doing everything you can to avoid, run from, or even ignore what you feel inside. You think, *Maybe it will go away.* You might dull the discomfort with drugs, alcohol, shopping, plastic surgery, or anything else that will take away your attention from the hardships of life. The problem is, much of this discomfort comes from inside. Like an alarm clock, pain alerts you to changes you need to make in your actions, values, and motivations. When you're faced with the prospect of having to do something that contradicts who you are, the discomfort and anxiety you feel inside are the red flags that direct your course of action.

Do you learn as much from experiencing pain as you do from experiencing pleasure?

Let's say, for example, you are a senior manager in a large corporation, and your boss tells you that you need to select one or two underachievers to let go. "Choose wisely," your boss warns. "You wouldn't want one of your junior staff taking your job." You might hear this as an invitation to get rid of someone you see as a threat to your position. As you look over the group you manage, you notice one person who has exceeded expectations and may, in fact, be a direct threat to your job. As you consider the idea of laying off this staff member, you may find yourself in conflict. *Sure, this employee has done an excellent job, but I have to watch out for* my *family*, you tell yourself. This in turn, evokes two conflicting sets of business ethics—one that says greater productivity will come from this employee, who is best for the business and reflects positively on me, versus an ethic fueled by insecurity: *This person's performance is threatening my job.* The resolution of the conflict depends on how well you know yourself.

In this instance, your feelings, especially the uncomfortable ones (envy, fear of failure, fear of success), are sending you signals about what's right and wrong and forcing you to reengage the issue of who you are. How you respond to those signals depends on whether you have the gumption to face who you are, or whether you'll hide your head and further bury the deeper insights into the true you. Conflict—in this case, deciding who to fire—reveals your true inner self.

In this way, conflict (and subsequently pain and suffering) reveals who you truly are. The more you try to extinguish pain, the further away you'll be from this realization until you are past feeling, and no longer capable of picking up key clues into who you are.

Remember, it costs something to gain something. If you put very little into understanding yourself, you'll understand very little about yourself.

Feeling a Little Stressed?

How do you usually react to pressure, stress, and anxiety? Do you tend to have headaches or other aches and pains on difficult days? Do you have tightness in your chest or problems breathing? Do you get sad and cry uncontrollably, or lose your temper? Do you give in and give up very quickly even when you know you're right? Perhaps you simply hold it all in to avoid showing weakness, or become passively aggressive.

> THINK ABOUT HOW YOU USUALLY REACT TO PRESSURE, STRESS, AND ANXIETY. DO YOU FEEL THAT YOU REACT WELL?

During stressful periods, does it take you longer than normal to unwind at the end of the day? Do you roll into a little ball and disappear in a dark corner? Are you a pill popper? Do you have trouble falling asleep? Have you gained or lost weight? Have you become a couch potato, unable to find the energy or desire to do things with your significant other or your children? Are you drinking more than normal? Do you fail to exercise regularly? By now you may feel like a bobblehead doll!

Because business people are subject to so much stress, it's appealing to think it all comes from outside sources. That's because the task of identifying the internal causes of stress seems so formidable. As we said earlier, your response to pain, anxiety, and stress supplies clues to who you are. Even in stressful situations, major discomfort may come from a core life stressor within—the difference between how you view yourself and the expectations others have of you.

You may feel that you lack the ability to accurately identify these internal sources of tension, but almost everyone has the capacity to do so to some degree, at least some of the time. To get to your core, you must pay attention to your life's stresses and strains, and especially take note of how you react to them.

Face the Mirror

The point is that you can't truly know who you are until you address the feelings you have about the traits that make up who you are. Taking each attribute in turn, you must identify, assess, and understand how you see yourself through your own eyes. Oftentimes you may find that you don't take the time to think about these things. As suggested earlier, introspection is becoming rarer and rarer. It's not that you are losing the ability to look deeply into your own feelings about who you are. It is that you lack the desire or willingness to do so, and fear may play a role because you are afraid of what you will see. You may find yourself focusing on other people's lives—their issues, and their dramas—in order to keep from facing the mirror and focusing on yourself, which also may keep you from becoming who you really wish to be.

There's a classic scene in the movie *The Neverending Story* in which the boy-hero Sebastian goes out on a quest that will test his every capacity and ability. Beforehand he is warned that greater men have failed miserably. Courageously accepting the challenge, he makes it through the first set of tests, escaping virtually unharmed, but certainly not unshaken. He then arrives at a mirror in which he must face the truth about himself. "Braver men have fled the mirror crying and screaming," he is warned. As he approaches the mirror, he looks inside and sees the true representation of himself—a harrowing image of the grief-stricken hero of the fantasy world in which he finds himself. Instead of shrinking from this image, he stands up tall and walks into the mirror, accepting not only who he is, but taking responsibility for who he is to become.

This is how you truly discover who you are. You must not only ask yourself, *What do I see when I see me?* but you must also look deeply into yourself and ask, *How do I feel about what I see when I see me?* It's crucial that you identify how you feel about who you are and accept yourself for all your faults and imperfections. You must take responsibility for what you have and wish to become.

Dig Up Your Past: Discovering the Archaeology of Your Identity

Speaking of movies, we can learn something from the popular movie character, Indiana Jones. Professor by day, Nazi-fighting artifact seeker by night, Dr. Jones makes digging up dead things exciting. In each adventure, he uncovers the secrets of the past in the relics he earnestly seeks. Whether it is a sacred chalice from Christianity's earliest days or an important monument worshipped by ancient tribes, Indy always knows the value that the past puts on each historical artifact. Standing behind his mantra, "This belongs in a museum!" he risks his life to guard the relics of the past, in effect, dedicating his life to keeping the past present.

You might see the Indiana Jones saga as a fantastic Hollywood adventure without seeing much relevance to your own life, but there is a connection. Whether you know it or not, your own archaeology—the history of who you are and how you developed the traits you identified earlier—directly influences who you are today. And in some cases, you may even be risking your life just to keep it intact.

Your identity is inextricably connected with your heritage, including the values, experiences, and personalities passed down from one generation to the next. What is your heritage? Who are your ancestors? How did *they* cope and how do *you* cope?

While we're discussing movies, here's another one. There's a memorable scene in the movie *Hitch* in which Alex Hitchins (played by Will Smith) sets up a romantic morning excursion for himself. To make it a deeply enriching activity, he takes his date to Ellis Island, where he has found the name of her first ancestor to step foot in America, and has opened the book of immigrants to the page featuring the ancestor's name. Yes, Hitch has done his homework. But what he doesn't know is that the ancestor was a thief and has brought extreme shame to the family. With her shameful ancestor's name in front of her, Hitch's date breaks into tears and runs out of the building sobbing.

What was your ancestors' port of entry? How did they get along with others? How many of their attitudes are you still living with today? What's the archaeology of your own identity? Your identity largely comes from your heritage. The stories, experiences, characteristics, attitudes, and traits that are passed down from one generation to the next provide the context in which you are born, and in which your identity is formed. A significant element of understanding and accepting who you are is discovering how your roots affect the way you act.

There are three ways your past determines who you are:

1. Your family history, passed down from generation to generation, sets up a context in which you act.
2. Your early childhood memories form the basis of your perspective and reasoning, and provide another context in which you act.
3. Your family's expectations dictate the initial boundaries you set on your own life, establishing a third context in which you act.

Your past provides at least three contexts for your actions. Of course, there's no guarantee that all of the contexts will be in agreement. In fact, it's far more likely that there will be conflicts among the three.

Family History: Swinging on the Branches of Your Family Tree
Family histories, including stories about nearly and dearly departed ancestors, hold a special place in your identity creation. The stories of grandparents and great-grandparents—their struggles, their lifestyles, their successes and failures—can form deep personal impressions, especially inasmuch as they represent strongly held family values, morals, and standards.

Perhaps you've gotten the "we had to walk to school barefoot . . . in the snow . . . uphill both ways" lecture from the older members of your extended family. As funny as they may be, such stories mean more to who you are than you might imagine: they invariably form a part of your sense of hard work and what it means to survive.

Let's say, for example, you've been reared in a hard-working upper middle-class home whose financial stability is built on the hard manual labor and dedication of your grandparents and great-grandparents. This may translate into valuing an honest, hard-earned dollar over anything else. On a superficial level, you may respond by choosing occupations that require you to put your muscle and sweat into making a living—a soft, cushy job may seem downright sinful. More profoundly, however, the image can have a deeper impression and may affect your sense of self by dictating that nothing that requires less than your blood, sweat, and tears is worthy. You may go from experience to experience doing things the hard way, because that's what validates an endeavor.

Early acquired concepts, like heritage, stay with you. You use what's useful and tend to discard or put in abeyance those things that you believe conflict with your life situations. Your family history can make an indelible mark on who you are, for better or for worse. The stories that are passed down can teach enduring values, but they can also lock you into a suit of armor.

Your recollections may be chock full of heroic figures who changed fate with a single action (a punch, a pitch, a heroic deed, and so on). You may, for example, have an ancestor who risked his or her life to save someone else. As a result, you may be inclined to serve others. On the negative side, however, you may be so inclined to sacrifice that you forego personal needs like understanding your personality and improving your own behavior because you consider it selfish, thanks to your life saving ancestor.

While such heroic figures and the enduring values they instill can be a force for good in your life, they can also create a false sense of self and a weak foundation for building your own identity. It's natural, and almost inevitable, that as you seek to hold true to the images and stories from an earlier era you create an inaccurate reality. There is a discrepancy between who your ancestors were and how they functioned in their world and who you are and how you function in today's world. Because of that difference, you can't simply claim, "If it worked for them, it will work for me!"

Most importantly, however, focusing too heavily on the stories of your family's past, whether consciously or subconsciously, can lead you to miss important cues about your own personality. Your history does not determine your future, it only influences it, no matter how much you may look like your parents, grandparents, and ancestors.

The key here is to figure out which ancestral stories and values are helping you, and which ones are hindering you. Remember, you are your own person, and although ancestors have left you a significant heritage, problematic issues and perspectives are likely to come right along with the enduring virtues bestowed on you.

REFLECT ON YOUR FAMILY HISTORY. WHAT STORIES, FIGURES, AND PERSPECTIVES ARE STILL ALIVE AND WELL IN YOUR FAMILY? WHERE DO YOU SEE YOURSELF IN RESPECT TO THOSE STORIES AND PERSPECTIVES?

One cautionary note about having many of your personality traits and behavioral tendencies passed down is that they can predispose you to make the same mistakes your forebears made. But this doesn't have to be the case. Your great-grandfather may have been a fighter, senselessly taking every challenge head on—often to his own detriment—which has led down through the years to your own bravado in confronting every manager or supervisor who ever got in your way. Learn to use what works for you, today. Don't doom yourself to repeat the past.

By identifying antecedents of your personality, tendencies, and perspectives you can get a clearer understanding of why you have the perspectives that you do, and free yourself to use them to your advantage or set them aside. Let's stop for a moment and look at two people whose heritages have shaped them, and what happened as a result.

Victoria B. and her Mutiny

Victoria grew up in a loving working-class religious family in Chicago. Her father was a foreman at a local steel mill, and Victoria recalls the time that his boss retired, and rather than promoting Victoria's father, management hired a tough, hard-charging woman instead. She remembers how hard her father's new boss made him work, demanding long hours and excruciating perfection, while cutting his workforce by 10 percent.

As time went by, Victoria's father complained about his new boss and sometimes took his frustration out on his family. Not only was he constantly irritable, but he snapped at his wife and kids for the smallest infraction.

As you might imagine, Victoria's experience turned her into a little dictator on the job. Although a woman in a male-dominated industry, she is extremely successful, receives numerous promotions, and has just been elevated to vice president of finance. Senior executives love her because she is results oriented, runs a tight ship, and saves the corporation money year after year. Vicky is a "company woman" who patterns her management style after her boss: if something is going to be done right, it's best to do it yourself. Victoria walks the company line to an extreme that, as we'll see, causes trouble for her.

Victoria is a domineering team leader, micromanaging, openly berating her staff, and dreaded as a manager. She often bends the rules on her own authority, inventing new policies and practices without including her direct reports and team members. Despite the awards and generous bonuses, Vicky's team members and senior directors are frustrated, unhappy, and fearful of losing their jobs over the slightest mistake. Victoria has become the frustrating micromanager her father complained about years earlier.

On the eve of a company-wide Christmas party, Victoria receives a disturbing anonymous letter from one of her employees:

> *We gave a questionnaire to 150 people in the finance department, and on behalf of your team, we want to let you know that we've decided not to attend the Christmas party. No one feels like celebrating after being overworked and yelled at all year. Your refusal to be collaborative and to make us a real team means that many people are looking for ways to leave the department or company.*

Broadsided by this note, Victoria feels humiliated, betrayed, and enraged. The entire organization will see that *her* team is boycotting the event, and no doubt, the fingers will be pointed at her. Retreating to the ladies' room, shaking with anger and trying to gain control, Victoria sits in a stall for forty-five minutes trying to figure out her next move. Being a woman who is known for thinking fast on her feet and taking calculated risks, Victoria has had her feet knocked from underneath her. She is literally frozen in her tracks.

While this may have all come as a surprise to Victoria (she actually believed her employees were satisfied with their jobs and her leadership), she missed key cues that would have prevented such an embarrassing and humiliating situation—starting with her childhood experiences. Had Victoria paid attention to her upbringing, spending a little quality time on introspection, she would have been more sensitive and aware of her employees and those around her, and could have avoided such an embarrassing circumstance.

We can draw a direct line between Victoria's childhood and her professional downfall over issues of trust, power, and control. She learned from her father that the most effective way to get what she wants is to demand it. And while it may have worked for her father's boss, and even for her father at home, it spells certain crisis for her professional career. She tried to apply her father's personality and situation to her own case and discovered that because the workplace variables were different, so was the outcome.

Jimmy C., the Fighting Irishman
Jimmy, a thirty-five-year-old senior marketing manager, is of Irish decent. He grew up in a middle-class family with his two sisters and is the only child in the family to earn a college degree. Jimmy's family is close-knit, and his sisters had to sacrifice in order for him to get his diploma. As such, Jimmy feels the pressure to live up to expectations.

While at first he has quickly risen among the ranks in his organization, the pressure to perform is too great. Before long, he's smoking two packs of cigarettes per day.

What started as a promising career at age thirty stalls, and Jimmy feels as though he's barely holding on. He becomes increasingly blocked at work and no longer projects the sunny, confident demeanor that goes with the job.

Jimmy's problems continue for two years and show every sign of getting worse. He responds by looking to his Irish ancestry for inspiration and motivation. He comes up with figures like John L. Sullivan, Irish Bob Murphy (both boxers), and Tug McGraw (a baseball pitcher), who embody the one-man-against-the-world ethic. He is particularly fond of McGraw's "Ya gotta believe!" mantra. But his identification with these figures doesn't work for long.

Jimmy doesn't know that these are wish-fulfillment fantasies, overemphasizing the muscle power of individual men. All he knows is that, despite his attempts at self-motivation, he sinks further into depression. So he looks to other traditional Irish stereotypes and begins to drink, using images of hard-drinking and hard-swearing ancestors as his unconscious guide. The prospect of becoming regional manager not only disappears, but Jimmy soon loses his job, and is continuously intoxicated.

Jimmy refuses to look within himself, identify his problems, and shape his thoughts to free himself emotionally from the labels and expectations of his family and his misperceived Irish heritage. In other words, Jimmy is unable to make the life and work transitions required because of his inability to identify and deal with the family and social forces that form his life.

In the end, Jimmy forms his identity around his own faulty perspective of his heritage and his parents' expectations, without any regard to who he believes himself to be.

No amount of professional success can compensate for that failure. As Jimmy learns, family expectations and roles can have a powerful effect on who we are and how we act, especially when they differ from the roles and labels we may aspire to or may hold for ourselves.

WHAT FAMILY IMAGES, EXPECTATIONS, OR CHILDHOOD MEMORIES ARE YOU CARRYING INTO YOUR PERSONAL AND PROFESSIONAL LIFE? TAKE SOME TIME TO DISCOVER WHERE COMMON THEMES FROM YOUR CHILDHOOD MAY BE APPEARING IN YOUR DAILY LIFE.

Sandbox Memories: Digging for Answers

After family history, second, equally potent influencers of your identity are the rich memories from your childhood that may or may not be buried away in your "sandbox." Your first experiences in life are foundations from which you form your own perspectives. The stories and experiences of your childhood, including your family's assertions about you, often form the basis from which you act. Although it may seem that these experiences dim along with the rest of your conscious memories, they are never actually forgotten, but are stored in your unconscious. What happened to you when you were a child stays with you and, if not identified and put in context, may cause you to react reflexively in the same way as when you were a child. The past never leaves you, but tends to form your response, especially in stressful times. The individual stories we'll look at reinforce this point time and again.

Early sandbox memories contain healthy doses of parental assertions about who you are. Particular memories and enthusiasms that may have stood out in your early years may never have never completely gone away and may show up in your daily actions. For example, perhaps you lost a loved one as a child; today that past loss can make it hard to take risks with long-term consequences, such as making a midlife career change, marrying your longtime significant other, or moving to another state for a job change or promotion. There are many factors that affect your response in situations like these. Your childhood memories form a solid basis for understanding why you react the way you do.

There is a true story about a shark photographer who was featured on the Discovery Channel. Her first impulse when sharks approach her unprotected form is to freeze. Her second is to give in to fear and panic. Later, she recalls a small voice inside her saying, "I think I can! I think I can!" as she fights, claws, and swims her way to safety. In order to save her life, her inner resources harken back to an early motivational feeling she first encounters in the well-known children's tale "The Little Engine That Could." In the story, the little engine conquers seemingly impossible obstacles by believing and by repeating, "I think I can! I think I can!" to the rhythm of the wheels.

In particular, we often tend to resort to early memories to find comfort during times of trial, change, or crisis, especially when we're backed into a corner trying to find our way out. While this can occasionally be helpful, it usually isn't, as it can represent a form of turning away from the full impact of change. Let's say, for example, that you are a project manager for a major manufacturer and are in the process of getting the product out to distributors. Your product fails inspections and has to be recalled. While you may not have been directly connected with its manufacture, the failure falls on you as the project manager. When your senior manager blames you for the problem in loud and unflattering terms, how do you respond? Why do you respond like that? How similar is your reaction to childhood confrontations with teachers or parents?

In many cases, those of you who would find yourself fighting against the senior manager or vehemently arguing your case may have learned that reaction from childhood confrontations: if you argued loudly enough, the other kid would back down. For others, shrinking from confrontations and keeping quiet in the face of criticism (while harboring intense negative feelings inside) may be the continuation of a different childhood pattern. The problem with relying on childhood memories is that these images and experiences are usually inconsistent with your current reality, even if they had validity as a child.

No doubt you have childhood figures and memories that you summon when you need motivation, inspiration, or relief from adversity. The problem isn't that you've had these images to call upon, but that sometimes calling the "good ghosts" brings up the "evil ghosts." Do you save images that are incongruent with reality at best and linked to negative experiences from the past at worst? As you'll recall, Victoria B. did, and we all saw what happened to her.

To what extent are your current actions based on your ancestral family tree?

Are You Captive of Family Expectations?

Your childhood memories are rich with your own family expectations and ideals. A great deal of your childhood is filled with the hopes your family has for you as you grow—hopes that form undeniable impressions on who you are and who you become. Your family's expectations are some of the strongest influences in your life, and are difficult to ignore.

As you grow and mature, these expectations come into play in your various decisions and life experiences. In each situation, you may actually judge your reaction against what your family expects. As you get older, you may find that your family's expectations aren't realistic or don't represent what you desire for yourself. You may even find yourself fighting against your family's expectations. Unbeknownst to you, however, the tension from the inconsistencies between your parents' ideals and your own are too profound to bridge even with the "comfort figures" of your family's past. You have to identify and understand your family's expectations for you, your expectations for yourself, and where the two either interconnect or contradict each other.

Affirming aspects of who you are often will require that you affirm acquired values against family values or beliefs. What do you do when you find yourself in a sticky situation at work? Do you explain your way out of things? Do you freeze? Do you fight back?

Getting Past Your Past

In any examination of who you are, what you value, and the basis of your own perspective, it is important to note that where you come from determines, in part, who you are. Yet this idea is not so simple as the old maxim, "The apple doesn't fall far from the tree." While families and forbears sometimes have a direct influence on such things as your identity, choice of career, and degree of success, the past often influences the future in a more complex manner. Many American success stories illustrate a less direct influence: children who grow up to exceed the limits of their ancestors' socioeconomic levels. Some of you spend your entire lives fighting the ideals and accepted norms and images that lie at the root of your family tree.

In other words, more often than not it's your *reaction* to your roots, childhood, and family expectations that makes the difference. What perceptions have you accepted as your own? Which ones are you striving to erase? Here are four steps that will help you identify how your past is present in you, and how to get past your past.

1. Ask yourself, "Where do I come from?" Take a few moments to think about what has influenced who you are. Explore your family tree and take advantage of all of your family members' oral histories and any Web sites, journals, and research materials that may prove useful. What circumstances did they live in? Is there a common theme or perspective to their opinions or reactions?

Now think about the experiences of your childhood. Go as far back as you possibly can and identify what memories, experiences, and circumstances might still be alive and well in your life. How did you respond to stressful situations then? How do you respond now? Do you see a common thread between the two?

Next, think about the expectations your family had or has for you. How are they evident in your own pursuits and endeavors?

2. Put family experiences into an appropriate context. Whether it's your ancestors' trials and tribulations, your childhood experiences, or your family's expectations for you, they all need to be considered in their own relevant contexts. For example, the obstacles your forbearers overcame may be completely unrelated to what you go through today. The same goes for your childhood experiences and family expectations. What kinds of conditions and circumstances do you find in your family's past? In your own past? How do they relate to what you experience today? What traits and characteristics helped you and your family survive and be successful?

3. Bring it all to the present. Once you've identified the perspectives and values that characterized these past dilemmas, issues, and experiences, take a moment to analyze how they have been translated into your life today. Are these traits and characters still evident? Compare and contrast their circumstances with what you face today. How do you see their perspectives reflected in your own opinions and behavior? Do you use a certain emotional strategy to get your way that may have been apparent in your past, or that of your family?

4. Keep the useful, toss the inappropriate. Assessing the family traits you have identified against what you face today, what works and what doesn't? Find the inconsistencies between your past and your present and see how your past may not be working for your present. You may have personality styles or behaviors that clash with your current environment and circumstances—traits that worked in the past, but don't necessarily work for you now. What about your past makes you confident and proud to be who you are? What doesn't? Choose the characteristics you believe will serve you well in the long run, and discard those that won't.

Recognizing your core self is a challenging task because it involves facing unpleasant feelings. But the compensation is that you're equally likely to encounter pleasant memories, wonderful feelings, and the times in your past when you've felt greater freedom. These are the treasures from your personal history that help you understand with confidence the person you are.

Action Items
- Challenge your preconceived notions.
- Flex your mental muscles by reflecting on who you think you are and who you truly want to be.

Chapter 2: What's in YOUR Label Box?

We do not deal much in facts when we are contemplating ourselves.

—Mark Twain, American humorist and author (1835–1910)

Step Two: Resolve Contradictions
IDENTIFY YOUR ROLES AND LABELS. TRY TO RESOLVE THE CONTRADICTIONS BETWEEN WHO YOU BELIEVE YOURSELF TO BE AND WHO PEOPLE THINK YOU ARE (THIS PROCESS LEADS TO AN IDENTIFICATION AND ALIGNMENT OF YOUR AUTHENTIC SELF).

Labels can have a powerful influence on what you become. Canon advertises its cameras by insisting, Image is Everything, while Sprite soda declares, Image is Nothing. Thirst is Everything. Popular mainstream culture encourages you to fit into boxes or molds—rebel, liberal, iconoclast, slowpoke, careless driver, dumb blonde—even as it teaches you to break free of the molds of the past. The point is, you want to know where you fit in, even if it means donning a label that might not actually fit.

People and organizations assign you labels all the time based on their expectations and assumptions about you. Some of them fit, and some don't. Labels can be encouraging and also hurtful. They can make you feel like an insider or an outsider. Sometimes they can lead you toward an identity you really can't (or don't want to) or shouldn't assume, but you force yourself to wear that mismatched label so at least you know where you fit into the external environment.

For a great example of the power and pitfalls of labels, we turn to that matchless chronicler of human psychology, Dr. Seuss, and his classic tale about the Star-Bellied Sneetches. Those Sneetches who have "stars upon thars" are considered the cream of the crop, while the blank-bellied Sneetches on the beaches are left out and feel inferior. A savvy salesman visits the Sneetches and, recognizing the opportunity to make a quick buck, offers to put stars on those without, and does so. By the end of the day, the Sneetches discover—at some cost—that it isn't the stars that determine their worth, but what is on the inside that truly matters. What an exercise in the often infantile and ephemeral nature of labels!

Dr. Seuss's Sneetches are a perfect example of the incredibly ridiculous things any of us may do to try to fit a label or image. Paying attention to the labels you carry is crucial to understanding why you behave the way you do, and how you may be getting in your own way both at work and in life. Every day you face the conflict of either trying to live up to, or altogether avoid, a label given to you, whether it fits or not. The greater truth is that the label-induced contradictions you live with and don't know how to resolve eventually hamper your own success. Let's look at a couple of stories that help clarify the point.

"Don Juan" de Carson

Carson fondly remembers going to magic shows as a child. Boy, was he amazed with the handsomely dressed man who put a beautiful lady in a box, spun her around a few times, said a few magic words with fancy hand movements, and—before the mesmerized audience knew it—made the lady disappear! As Carson chuckles about fooling his childhood friends with his magic tricks, he now sees that his friends often knew what the trick was, but didn't want to see the reality—and that's magic. Today, Carson lives his life fooling not only others, but himself as well. He doesn't realize he's a smoke-and-mirrors guy. You know the type—people who appear one way but in reality are the exact opposite. On the outside, Carson is a dashing and intelligent forty-something. A handsome, polished professional, he is a Don Juan with the ladies and other men envy him for his good looks and charming ways.

What people don't know about Carson is that he has trouble dealing with women. If he can't hypnotize them with his charisma, he maligns them or totally avoids them. So on the inside, Carson is disturbed by his inability to relate to women. He's able to hide the problem behind his Don Juan label until he takes this image too far.

As a senior manager in a multibillion-dollar mutual fund company, Carson is proud of his leadership authority and enjoys being in control. In his dating, he chooses women who are amiable and nonresistant. He enjoys being with women who know their place and are easily dominated.

In fact, Carson often jokes that all women should be dominated, whether educated, uneducated, rich, or poor (his version of "barefoot, pregnant, and in the kitchen"). But because of his Don Juan label, most people laugh off his opinions. From his limited perspective, this label renders him invulnerable to any meaningful recourse.

It also helps that Carson never speaks about his personal views in the workplace—until one unforgettable day. While having lunch with a female direct report, Carson receives a call on his cell phone. Excusing himself, he takes the call and, in the course of the conversation, reveals his view of women in the workplace. Forgetting he is still in the presence of his female colleague, Carson exclaims, "I'm sick of these women who think just because God gave them the sense to obtain an education they should be sitting right beside us men running corporations. Why can't they be like my mother, someone who knows her place and doesn't fight it?"

This doesn't sit well with his luncheon companion, and she demands an explanation. Carson turns red and tries to dig himself out, but the damage is done. Before he knows it, a new label has been affixed to him like a scarlet letter. In an instant, he goes from "Don Juan" to "male chauvinist," and despite his apologies, including the formal letter of apology he is forced to write by the director of human resources, Carson can't escape this new label. After the incident, Carson receives poor evaluations from his superiors and never receives another promotion, although he never sees the connection between his demeaning opinion and his failure to advance in the workplace.

That's how it often goes with labels. Once you've been living with them and responding to them long enough, they skew your perspective of what is appropriate and what is inappropriate. As it is with Carson, if you spend enough time enjoying the labels you've assumed or acquired, you lose sight of the negative responses that labels might incur, leading to the prospect of serious mistakes at work and in life. You may also lose sight of which labels fit and which don't.

The irony of Carson's experience is that the Don Juan label he has been reveling in is actually nothing more than a nicer side of male chauvinism. The moment it leads him to inappropriate actions, he slides from one label down to another, and is forever branded as a sexist.

But no matter how innocent they appear, labels can seriously damage an unsuspecting person's career.

Jason and His Forgotten Reservation

Jason is a thirty-something Native American who works as a regional vice president of sales for a global computer giant. Reared on a reservation in Oklahoma, Jason was taught the value of hard work, living a clean life, and in particular, the important role of women in the home. Jason was taught specifically to honor and sustain the women in his life. However, that respect is for women in traditional roles.

His father's ongoing speech to Jason is, "Our women must be good wives, and must always understand that their calling is to help us. Get a wife who wants to stay at home. Too much worldly ambition can be detrimental." Jason loves and honors his parents. His father is a kind and gentle spirit who has good intentions. Jason faithfully transfers his father's lessons into the workplace and the resulting misapplication is disastrous.

At work, the team of directors that Jason manages respects him for his creativity and vision. Jason takes good care of his team, making sure they have every resource in order to exceed their goals; his senior executives praise him for his success.

Though Jason appears enthusiastic and hardworking on the outside, he has serious trouble dealing with the opposite sex because he has improperly transferred his father's teachings about women to the workforce. Because he feels that a woman's place is in the home, he treats women as though they don't belong at work, and tends to show them little respect in very subtle ways.

During a meeting one day, he notices that one of his female directors is pouring a cup of coffee for herself. Seemingly in jest, Jason stops her and chuckles, "Why don't you be a good girl and pour a cup for me?" Shocked and embarrassed at the sudden silence in the room, the woman leaves the room without saying anything.

Before the afternoon is over, however, Jason is served up with a letter from human resources and a meeting with his manager. And then Jason is slapped with an investigation and the label of sexual harasser.

Jason is absolutely blindsided by this charge and corresponding label. After all, he was taught by his father that such behavior is okay. Because his colleagues had constantly laughed at his antics and no one tried to stop him, Jason actually made no effort to distinguish between home and work. In the end, Jason makes a lateral move and ends up reporting to a woman. He should not have applied his reservation-based labeling to the workplace.

Unlike Carson's missteps, Jason's inappropriate actions stem more from the labels he has for others, rather than the labels he has assumed for himself. The way we label others can come back to haunt us, especially if it means treating others with less respect and dignity. It's crucial, then, to take a serious look at the way you apply the labels you acquired at home and the labels you give to others. Identifying where your home labels and workplace labels clash is essential to your success.

Jason's problems begin at home, through the labels he is taught and his experiences pertaining to women. While he is taught to respect women in their place, he inappropriately applies that limited respect (limited by place and time) to the workplace, and reaps the harvest of the lesson that "home cooking" is not workplace fare.

So unlike Carson, Jason's inappropriate actions at work stem more from the labels he has for others, rather than the labels he has assumed for himself. While you may not have problems treating the opposite sex appropriately, the lesson may apply in other ways. The way we label others can come back to haunt us, especially if it means treating others with less respect and dignity.

Therefore it's crucial to take a serious look at the way you may be applying the labels you acquired at home, and the labels you are giving to others. Identifying where your home labels and workplace labels clash is essential to your success.

Look at Your Labels: Your Expectations Versus Everyone Else's

With its memorable and witty *What's in your wallet?* slogan, Capital One asks you to take a closer look at what you're really carrying with you, which it hopes will be one of its credit cards. But your wallet isn't the only thing you carry around with you all the time. Throughout your life, you carry labels and roles that determine how you behave.

Years ago at a health center in New Jersey, Claude decided he'd try an exercise in labeling. He set up several boxes containing labels that the staff could wear at their choosing. Labels included *Caucasian*, *Black*, *social worker*, *psychologist*, *physician*, and *nurse*. As it turned out, many staff members picked up labels that did not fit them. Some Blacks identified themselves as Caucasians, some social workers labeled themselves as doctors, and some nurses chose tags as psychologists. The trend was to reach for what they considered higher-ranking labels, even though they clearly didn't fit. Many staff members seemed uncomfortable parading around with them.

At first blush, you might say these people must have been crazy. In reality, they were unhappy with their actual labels and trying to upgrade.

Clearly roles and labels have powerful effect on who you are and how you act. Without understanding which roles and labels you're carrying around, you are likely to face some frustrating conflict. Before we start sorting through your label box with you, let's do a little sociology 101 lesson on roles.

Forgive the socio-babble—a *role* to us psychological researchers is an interactive, socially prescribed set of behaviors that comes from one's situation or position in the world. In other words, roles are a way of behaving according to the situation you're in. That means they're always changing. For example, at home you may be a mother or father or cousin. At work, you may be an executive, manager, or a subordinate. The role you're in changes along with your environment. You must or should take on different roles at work than you do at home.

ARE YOU A BETTER WIFE OR HUSBAND THAN MANAGER OR
SUBORDINATE? ARE YOU A BETTER BROTHER OR SISTER
THAN YOU ARE A PEER OR TEAM LEADER? WHY?

While understanding traditional roles like father, sister, and so forth is helpful to understanding who you are, there's nothing you can really do to alter them. Work roles, though, are a different story.

For example, my research shows that both gender and race affect work roles in corporate America. According to the research, 75 percent of women felt less connected, less empowered, and less involved in the decision-making process than men. Ninety-five percent of women felt that they faced a glass ceiling or concrete ceiling in their organizations, compared with only 12 percent of men. These results tell us that women workers believe their *woman* label brands them as inferior to men in the workplace. But that's not all.

Most male respondents (95 percent) indicated that their superiors provided them and their peers with the budget and resources to perform successfully. Men also felt that they received critical projects to ensure their visibility and upward movement. However, 90 percent of men felt that formulating policy was not critical to their organizational role. Nevertheless, a majority of men (91 percent) felt that they had the authority and decision-making power to determine their own success.

Women disagreed with men at an alarming rate. Sixty percent of women did not feel that they or their female peers received the budget or resources necessary to successfully perform, nor did they feel that they were awarded critical projects to ensure their visibility and upward movement. Eighty percent of women felt that formulating policy was critical to their role within the organization, which greatly differs from the male perspective. Only 50 percent of the women felt that they were given sufficient authority and decision-making power to determine their own success. As a program manager who has been with her current employer for over ten years stated,

> *It's always been said that if you handle the money, you have the power. Many of us do not deal with budgets, and we again must seek out positions and ways to learn how to work with budgets. That's where the power lies, and we as women don't have that power.*

These results indicate an inappropriate application of traditional roles in the workplace: men at the office (like traditional fathers) handle the money and make the rules, and the women (like traditional wives and daughters) meekly follow their lead.

While the battle rages on between men and women to equalize roles in the workforce, confronting these inequalities doesn't immediately help you understand and improve who *you* are individually. So let's turn to something you can change on your own, or at least directly affect—labels.

Unlike roles, labels are relatively easier to define *and* change. Labels are simply outward reflections of who you are. They can be how others see you, or how you see yourself. Unlike roles, labels don't change from situation to situation—they just stick to you. Most importantly, labels don't necessarily direct your behavior in the same way roles do, which makes them easier to work with.

Remember our friends at the New Jersey Health Center who got to choose their own new labels? That exercise was a prime example of people taking on labels that don't fit. Often the result is that they do strange and even ridiculous things. While the New Jersey Health Center exercise may be an extreme example of inappropriate labeling, you can have just as much trouble with mislabeling that is far more subtle. Are some of the things that you have done, that seem in retrospect, inexplicable, the result of label-induced conflict?

Controlling your labels rather than letting them control you is crucial to your success. To control your labels, you must take three steps.

1. Open your box of labels: are they useful or harmful? You have your very own box full of labels, some of which fit and some of which don't. What's in it?

Caucasian, Black, black sheep, problem child, smart, naïve, blue-collar, white-collar, Republican, Democrat, liberal, conservative, overachiever, aggressive, power hungry, political—anything you or other people use to define you is a label. While labels are not necessarily bad, they often are. Labels don't change according to the setting and, most significantly, are not interactive. In fact, they are often restrictive and inhibit interaction. In the worst cases, people deal with the label and completely forget about the living, breathing human being behind it. (For example, during the Vietnam War, American soldiers used the label *Charlie* to identify a Viet Cong enemy as a nonperson with whom the only appropriate interaction was killing.) There were other more disagreeable labels (slope and gook, for example).

The oldest labels in your box come to you from others, starting with your family. Whether they're accurate or not, they can have a strong effect on you and your interactions. Remember that labels don't have to influence your behavior but, in fact, they often do. Turning to them in a crisis is sometimes helpful, but more often, reverting to labels can effectively paralyze you, taking away the very flexibility you need to survive (as happened with Jimmy C. in the previous chapter).

One of the biggest problems with labels is they often have incredible staying power. If you've ever actively fought a misassigned label, you know what we're talking about. Take a label like *incompetent*. It only takes one or two flubs on the job to get this label firmly glued to your shirt. "Hi, my name is Incompetent"! And once it's stuck there, it's awfully hard to get off.

We've already noted that not all labels are demeaning or personally damaging. Some can be quite beneficial and even vital to your success. Furthermore, labels may function differently in different places. For example, growing up with the label of *smart* may serve you well in the family, while the label of *industrious* may help you more in the workplace.

WHAT LABELS ARE YOU CARRYING? WHICH ONES EMPOWER YOU? WHICH ONES WANT TO MAKE YOU GIVE UP?

All in all, labels tend to fall into two contrasting stacks: useful and useless, or helpful and harmful. The trick is to find and utilize the useful and helpful and reject the useless and harmful labels.

Useful and helpful labels are those that truthfully reflect your actions and values. For example, you may believe it's important to act with integrity on the job, so that what you say and do reflects that belief. In response, your coworkers and clients label you as *honest*, a label you want to reinforce.

Useless and harmful labels are those that have a negative effect on your interactions with others and, most important, conflict with an inner sense of who you are. Tweaking our example a little, too zealous an expression of moral values and too vigorous an espousal of integrity can earn you labels of *self-righteous* and *judgmental*. Even if you aren't really that way, suddenly you're labeled as such. Labels are not created in a vacuum; they're specific to a particular context and can't be safely carried elsewhere. A brushback pitcher—one who throws intentionally close to a batter to make him step back from the pitch—may be a good father and safe driver just as easily as he might be a habitual jerk. Off the baseball field, his baseball label is irrelevant. Once again, letting your emotional intelligence do some work is key to success in reconciling helpful and harmful labels.

REVISIT THE LABELS YOU HAVE IDENTIFIED. TRY TO DECIDE WHICH ARE HELPFUL AND HARMFUL.

2. Classify your labels, from home to your five o'clock shadow. You're not born with labels. Even the oldest labels you've carried from childhood—*bully, spoiled, sensitive, smarty-pants, goody two-shoes, pushover*—didn't come with you at birth, though it may feel like they did. Understanding where they came from and how impermanent they actually are is a necessary and beneficial starting point. You get labels from different environments, from your earliest life setting (family) to your most recent life situations.

Home is Where the Labels Are

The oldest labels comprise images attributed to you by others with the family. Early in life you take on many labels. You are born either a son or daughter (labels as well as roles), and from then on you invariably acquire labels according to your behavior. These labels may be assigned because of behaviors that have a short life and are expected to change (*crybaby* or *bed wetter*), or they may include expectations your family holds for you (*daddy's girl, momma's boy, intelligent, shy, prissy, mature competitor, old for her age*).

REVISIT THE LABELS YOU HAVE IDENTIFIED. PAY PARTICULAR ATTENTION TO THE ONES YOU HAVE BEEN CARRYING SINCE CHILDHOOD. THESE HAVE PROBABLY BEEN ASSIGNED TO YOU BY YOUR FAMILY. HAVE YOU LEFT OUT ANY?

Your family labels may apply only within your family, but they can be complex and defining (*loner, hard worker, rebel, happy, troublesome*). The problem is that while labels shouldn't be carried out of their creation context, they tend to be anyway, and so often travel into other environments.

Family-assigned labels are often the most difficult to come to terms with because they are so imbedded in your deepest and earliest memories and experiences that they may seem part of who you truly are.

What is Your Frame of Reference?

Everyone has a reference group. Your family, neighborhood, friends, associates, church, and social groups are all places you turn to for reference or meaning in your life.

This concept of a *reference group* is somewhat complex, but for the purpose of this book we'll call it a group that reflects your ideas of various social expectations. Everyone goes through life with an internalized reference group with whom he or she identifies in terms of origins, experience, and, more rarely, aspirations. This group acts like a little voice inside our heads, letting us know how we measure up. Its basic message is always "Don't leave us!" But the individual most often hears "Danger! Don't stray too far away from us!" for your own safety.

Reference groups often dictate your sense of purpose and measure your success. You give them this power by paying attention to them; hence, reference groups end up as potent judges of the labels you carry.

Problems arise, however, when conflicting reference groups interpret and judge your labels differently. How your friends perceive you differs from how your family perceives you. *Rebel* may go over big with your friends, but may be a huge negative to your family, and an absolute disaster in the workplace. Endless numbers of television shows deal with the conflict teenagers face because of the difference between their friends' perceptions and that of their parents. Inevitably, they side with their friends because they like the labels available to them from that reference group more than those offered by parents.

Regardless of where the conflicts arise, you usually weigh the differences between the labels of your respective reference groups and come up with some kind of behavioral amalgam to minimize the conflict. As you can imagine, this is a recipe for great confusion and internal discord.

The sum of reference group pressures and their contradictory labels determine your criteria for success and your beliefs about whether or not and under what circumstances other people will accept you. Either way, the labels you accept from various reference groups can limit your growth to what is derived from the expectations of others.

How do your peers see you? Which of your labels are reinforced by your associates?

Your Five o'Clock Shadow

Hard worker, *social butterfly*, *lazy drifter*, and even *the boss* are examples of labels in the workplace. Like the nametag the waiter wears saying *Hi, my name is Ed*, you wear your workplace labels from eight to five, Monday through Friday. In fact, some people never put them down; they're shadowed by them after five o'clock and beyond. Regular business hours already take up the biggest chunk of your day; thanks to modern communications technology, your workplace labels may be spilling over into your personal life, wreaking unexpected havoc with whom you think you are. Labels such as *last-minute savior*, or the *fix-it person* describe someone that people in the workplace feel they can run to in a time of crisis. Does this work for you? Along with the many workplace labels for individuals, some labels like, *entrepreneurial, collaborative*, or *hierarchical* suggest behavior for the corporate culture as a whole.

Look for examples at the infamous Enron Corporation during its heyday. Its corporate culture favored fast-paced, innovative, and incredibly complicated financial transactions. Despite the fact that it had begun as a natural gas company in Nebraska and had grown for many years chiefly by operating power plants and pipelines, Enron viewed its culture as *entrepreneurial* and *competitive*. Lots of managers started adapting those labels for themselves, even though there was nothing in their background or experience to suggest they actually had these characteristics. In the end, the behaviors resulting from mislabeling and inappropriate role acceptance embedded in the self-described *fast-paced culture*—accompanied by selfishness, ruthlessness, and malfeasance—led to the complete collapse of a $111 billion company in two years. What *Fortune* magazine heralded as "America's Most Innovative Company" six years in a row turned out to be sadly mislabeled as such.

Having said that, it's important to realize that labels in the workplace aren't always bad. Oftentimes you model your workplace conduct and goals after others close to you or those working in your industry or profession. To some extent, role modeling and subscribing to labels can be constructive and can help you advance. But as we've seen, the process can be destructive if you engage in it indiscriminately and without regarding your own inner and early acquired values.

3. Check your labels at the door: did your roles and labels ever fit? More often than not, you take on different labels when you walk into new situations. When you're at work, recognize your work labels; when you're at home, trade the work identifiers for a home set. If you don't change labels—because you can't, or you won't, or you don't know how—the result could prove detrimental to you in both areas.

---✦---

WHEN YOU WALK INTO A DIFFERENT SITUATION, WHAT LABELS DO YOU CHECK AT THE DOOR? WHAT LABELS GIVE YOU TROUBLE WHEN YOU TRY TO UNLOAD THEM?

---✦---

Here's a scenario that shows how work labels can spill over into the rest of life in an unhealthy way. Darren and Rhonda, who work together and are also engaged, are playing Truth or Dare with friends. The other players dare Rhonda to use a metaphor to describe Darren. She thinks for a minute and answers, "Darren runs our relationship the same way he manages his team at the office: like a numbers cruncher." Then Darren gets the same dare to describe Rhonda. After pondering a minute, he says, "Rhonda treats her employees like children, and she treats me the same way. She's a mother hen." Whenever you check into a different environment, it's probably best to check your other labels at the door like you'd check your coat and hat.

Labels that never fit

We've seen how each of your personal environments has its own set of labels. But what happens when some of your roles and labels never fit anywhere to begin with? What happens when a label or perception someone has about you is completely at odds with how you perceive yourself?

It's hard to shed an inaccurate label, whether it came from you or someone else. The tragic story of Kurt Cobain, the former lead singer for Nirvana who took his own life in 1994, was a stark example of the difficulty of living with labels that don't fit. In a whirlwind turn of events, Kurt Cobain found himself at the front of a revolution in music, and his band, Nirvana, at the top of the charts. While most would revel in the newfound celebrity status, Cobain was unsettled and depressed. It turns out that he was uncomfortable with playing the part of a rock star—he didn't fit the role and didn't want the labels associated with being a musical icon. In the end, unable to resolve the conflict, Cobain took his life, but not before he left a revealing glimpse into the power of labels and the extreme conflict they can cause. In his controversial suicide note, Cobain reportedly explained:

> *I haven't felt the excitement of listening to as well as creating music along with reading and writing for too many years now. I feel guilty beyond words about these things. For example when we're back stage and the lights go out*

and the manic roar of the crowds begins, it doesn't affect me the way in which it did for Freddie Mercury, who seemed to love, relish in the love and adoration from the crowd which is something I totally admire and envy. The fact is, I can't fool you, any one of you. It simply isn't fair to you or me. The worst crime I can think of would be to rip people off by faking it . . . I'm too much of an erratic, moody baby! I don't have the passion anymore, and so remember, it's better to burn out than to fade away.[1]

Cobain's letter was the sad soliloquy of a gifted man who tragically failed to escape the labels that didn't fit him: he built his life around the way he thought others saw him, rather than the way he saw himself. Along the way he missed opportunities to express who he really was and become the man he wanted to be. Of course, not every instance of label conflict causes such a calamitous ending, but it does illustrate how harrowing your life can be if you're living with conflicting labels.

That is not to say that every instance of label conflict can cause such a calamitous ending, but it does illustrate how harrowing your life can be if you're living with conflicting labels. The great paradox of labels is that the more successful you are, the more you're at risk of becoming seriously encumbered by roles and labels that really don't fit. Contradictions among the labels from your family, society, the ones you've accepted for yourself, and the ones you've rejected can immobilize you. One of the reasons people tend to be inefficient and intolerant is because they're living with too many unidentified contradictions. Keeping these conflicts and contradictions at bay expends what therapists call *psychic energy*. The sense of that expenditure of energy often appears to you as anxiety.

So what do you do with accepted labels that are in conflict with your own sense of self? What's the price of trying to undo the internalization that has already taken place? The more you believe in the usefulness of the labels you wear, the more difficult it will be to change them.

REVISIT THE LABELS YOU HAVE PREVIOUSLY IDENTIFIED AND REFLECT AGAIN UPON THE ONES YOU THINK DON'T FIT WITH WHO YOU FEEL YOU ARE.

The process of change starts with getting back to who you believe you are on the inside. (Yes, here's that *emotional intelligence* thing again!) You need to be able to see past the layers of labels you have acquired throughout your life and pinpoint exactly who you believe you are.

The workplace labels reflect expectations, values, and demands that coworkers, managers, and bosses have with respect to you. Your inner beliefs about who you are may be closer to labels given early on by family and early experiences. Conflict occurs when the inner beliefs conflict with workplace expectations. The resulting mind-set is not usually helpful in the workplace or in social settings.

It is important to identify the many ways in which your roles and labels—individually and collectively—conflict with your own true sense of self. As earlier mentioned, keeping these conflicts under control expends mental energy. The internalization of labels with their contradictions and negative weights is a major cause of a feeling of discomfort and anxiety, and you're going to need mental energy and emotional intelligence to overcome those feelings. The worst-case scenario is when mental energy expended as anxiety is so great that you can't mobilize the necessary energy to put emotional intelligence to work for the task of sorting and reconciliation.

Clash of the Titans: Life Versus Work

While you'll find that your conflicting labels span numerous areas and situations in your life, you're also likely to find that the biggest conflicts come between early acquired labels and those you acquire at work. It shouldn't be too surprising that your greatest conflict comes from trying to reconcile these two most significant parts of your life.

The labels you acquire as a child tend to basically define you. They are associated with your earliest recollections and inevitably form a foundation for how you see yourself. However, as you learn and mature, you find yourself acquiring labels and handing out labels to others that contrast with what you learned at home. The conflict tends to come to a head at work, where you likely spend most of your day. That's what happened to Jason. Taught to be one way at home, he inappropriately transferred labels from that environment into his work life. And while, in the end his experience was similar to that of our friend Carson, Jason's problems stemmed from a more familiar source—the lessons he had learned at home, and his misinterpretation of those lessons in handing out labels to those around him.

Breaking Free and Breaking Through the Looking Glass

Sometimes, through no fault of your own, you find yourself assigned labels at work that don't fit you at all. This is often a result of others' perceptions of your experiences and behavior, but they can also come from others' preconceived notions about your race and gender. The research I've conducted only confirms what Jason and Carson both learned the hard way: gender and race lead to workplace labels that are unfair, burdensome, and seriously flawed.

THINK ABOUT THE LABELS YOU HAVE (FOR YOURSELF AND OTHERS) THAT YOU LEARNED IN CHILDHOOD. ARE YOU TRYING TO APPLY THEM IN THE WORKPLACE?

A focus group study involving only women found that women at work often feel considerable frustration from the conflict between who they are on the inside, and who they feel they have to be at work. Here's what some of the participants had to say.

- An executive director:

  The executive staff does not show me respect in meetings. I am overlooked or cut off when I am trying to express my opinion about critical issues impacting my department. I feel powerless and unfortunately I have to put up with this treatment, sue the company, or leave. If I leave, who is to say that it will be any better? You're damned if you do and damned if you don't.

- A vice president:

  My peers disrespect me by not bringing me in on certain pertinent discussions surrounding things that impact my department. My subordinates do not show me the proper respect when my superior is around by making jokes that really jab at me. I call them on it, and they say that they are only joking, and didn't mean any harm, but underneath it all, I know that they are attempting to make me seem incompetent. I have to stay on top of my game at all times and it is draining.

  Quite a few people feel their gender and race forces them into roles and labels at work that they're not comfortable with. For example:

- A corporate communications manager:

  My superior looks down on me. I don't know if it's due to my gender. He does not include me in crucial conversations that impact me or my department, and I am overlooked in other ways.

- A senior program manager:

  I interviewed with a male and he was rather condescending and arrogant . . . I still feel though that even though we [women] have the credentials, the education, and the experience that we are looked down upon in some manner as though people feel pity for us . . . People to this day will whisper and say things behind my back such as the company needed to fill a quota and this other person should have gotten the job instead of me.

The New Jersey Health Center exercise indicates that taking on inappropriate labels at work or playing parts that really don't fit may be a response to a sense of being disrespected. Such behavior is often destructive. My research indicates a sense of being disrespected is fairly common among women middle managers and senior executives, though not unknown among male executives.

If the Label Doesn't Fit, Dump it!

How do you dump the labels that don't fit?

First, identify the labels that conflict with your own sense of self. If you reject that group, do you feel adequately described by the remaining labels? Not too many of us will be satisfied by what we see at first. Separate the lot into labels to be discarded, and labels to be kept. Perhaps this may cause you to wonder how you got this set of labels in the first place. How do you categorize yourself? Have you ever thought of a person or course of conduct associated with a label and tried to model yourself accordingly? Do you always act the way that you think and feel? Clearly the latter is associated with spontaneity. When is it appropriate or justified?

IDENTIFY THE LABELS THAT CONFLICT WITH YOUR OWN
SENSE OF WHO YOU ARE.

One way to dump the labels you feel don't fit is to do the same for someone else. Think about the way others have been categorized or labeled. Do you know how the person got the label? Do you think the person is aware of the label? What bearing does the label have on the person's conduct? Which came first, the conduct or the label?

Try to use what you have learned from your own personal labeling process to treat this person differently. Take, for instance, a person who is reputed to have his or her job because of connections, not talent. Privately monitor your interactions with this person. Modify your behavior as if the person were a merit hire. Is there a change in the person's behavior? Please note that behavior on your part is scripted behavior. Are you comfortable with not being spontaneous?

Now, in terms of yourself, figure out which labels help and which labels hurt. Try seeing which ones you identify or agree with. Don't reject everything, just the labels that don't help. As you have already seen, you have to withstand some internal pressure for a while in order to change your habits and stop allowing others' expectations to define you. In the end, the labels you carry can inalterably impact your corporate performance, professional advancement, and your overall well-being, but it's up to you to decide which ones you'll accept, which you'll reject, and which ones you'll bestow on others, and most importantly, to determine what, if anything, you're going to do about it.

Action Items
- Identify your strongest workplace asset.
- Identify your major liabilities in the workplace.
- Identify how your personal and family history contributes to your strengths.
- Identify common themes from your childhood that appear in your everyday life.

Chapter 3: Taking the Risk

Every exit is an entry somewhere else.

—Tom Stoppard, British playwright (b. 1937)

Step Three—Embrace change; enable yourself and others

DO NOT STAND OPPOSED TO CHANGE; ACCEPT IT BY LEARNING TO TAKE APPROPRIATE RISKS. WORK TO UNDERSTAND AND ACCEPT DIFFERING CULTURAL CONTRIBUTIONS, AND FACILITATE WORKING WITH DIVERSITY. PARADOXICALLY, THIS FACILITATES SELF-UNDERSTANDING.

The next step in discovering Your Personal Power-Up is learning to embrace change while enabling yourself and others and taking appropriate risks. If you're dissatisfied with your career and your life, you have to be willing to change, to risk moving from the familiar to the unknown, decide to make to decisions in the future that are different from the kind of decisions you made in the past. Otherwise nothing will get better; without change and challenge you'll never grow. It's true that change can be frightening, and sometimes during a time of transition success and failure can feel the same. But change is coming whether we like it or not. Knowing how to handle it and take advantage of the opportunities it brings will keep you progressing forward.

You may recall the tale about Rip Van Winkle, an amiable but lazy farmer. He goes up into the mountains to get away from his complaining wife, falls asleep, and when he awakes, twenty years have gone by! When Rip goes back to his village, the entire place has changed. Going from house to house, he seeks out his wife, family, and old friends, only to find that they have all grown up and moved on. Finally he is recognized, and his daughter, long since grown and married, takes him to live with her. Rip discovers that the world had changed around him quite dramatically, but what he fails to realize is that he, too, has changed, so much that almost no one recognized him.

Like most literary tales, the story of Rip Van Winkle has a message, which is that we can't stop time, and failure to acknowledge change doesn't stop change from occurring. Perhaps you view change as something outside of yourself, something that happens around you and even to you, but not within. You tend to believe, erroneously, that you are relatively stable and consistent over time—that your own personalities and identities are the only constants in a sea of change. It's not you but the world around you that changes, and quite often these changes are not welcome. You may actually fight the movement towards change, and hold tight to the things you consider constant and essential. Just like Rip Van Winkle, we're all likely to recognize changes in the world around us without seeing change in ourselves.

Rarely do you see periods of social or cultural change as periods of personal change. Take, for example, the technology boom in America during the 1990s. You observed the change in corporate culture that ensued: dress codes, normal working hours, and the very idea of what working meant changed drastically during those years. Young, bright, and ambitious professionals flooded Silicon Valley as more traditional brick-and-mortar companies struggled to keep pace with the times. Wall Street lawyers and financiers mirrored the cultural changes as casual attire became the order of the day both at work and in New York's finest restaurants.

> PERHAPS YOU VIEW CHANGE AS SOMETHING OUTSIDE OF YOURSELF; SOMETHING THAT HAPPENS AROUND YOU AND EVEN TO YOU, BUT NOT WITHIN YOU. IF YOU DO, HOW IS THIS WAY OF THINKING IMPACTING YOUR CAREER AND PERSONAL LIFE?

But you might be thinking that's what happened *around* you, not *to* you. Yet as you consider more closely, even those of you who stayed in traditional industries far from the technological revolution were indelibly marked by it and the new ideas and patterns it brought to the corporate world. We now take for granted the speed and ease of digital and Internet communication, telecommuting, flexible office hours, and all the other innovations sparked by the technological boom. You probably experience work and think differently from the way you thought before the tech boom.

It's far easier to equate external change with internal change during periods of major personal upheaval or critical life crossroads. Marriage, the passing of a loved one, the birth of a child, the loss of a job, or promotion to a new job usually appear as a change on your personal radar screen because those outside experiences require internal transitions. You feel changed inside by the event; sometimes the change feels wonderful, and sometime it's filled with anxiety and unease. The huge number of books and articles on marriage, divorce, changing jobs, and the death of a loved one is evidence of this. We undergo a lifelong process of change in response not only to our own personal experiences, but to the changes we see in the social, cultural, and historical milieu. You are constantly adapting to the forces around you, both internal and external. And the more you fight change, the more antiquated you become and the more detrimental it is to your own personal growth.

It's crucial for you to recognize and accept the concept of change as a constant in order to enjoy success in your career and personal life. By ignoring change, you're liable to behave in a way appropriate to an earlier time, but not to today. These behaviors support a pattern of erroneous perception and feed into a cycle that becomes difficult to stop. In the end, much like the characters in the 1993 movie *Groundhog Day,* despite your daily interactions you inevitably awaken each morning to the same report on the clock radio. You have become stranded in time.

ARE YOU CONTENT WITH STAYING WHERE YOU ARE AND REMAINING THE SAME? DO YOU FEEL AS THOUGH YOU'RE STRANDED IN TIME? WHAT HAVE YOU DONE TO STOP REPEATING THE SAME BEHAVIORS OVER AND OVER AGAIN?

The Two Forces Within: Know Which One to Use

There are two primary forces inside you: the desire to remain the same and the desire to change. Let's call these *status quo* and *striving*, respectively. You are naturally inclined to favor one or the other. Status quo is supported by the influence of family, early peers, religious and social groups, and at first seem protective to the young and immature self, but leave a legacy of armoring and inflexibility, which can put sharp limitations on striving. When that influence imposes a heavy cost, as manifested by anxiety and immobility, you are dealing with a specialized part of the status quo force. We'll call this the *negative self*. The negative self is the ultimate anchor for status quo behavior.

A promotion or hiring of a new supervisor, manager, or executive at work invariably results in the institution of new directives, rules, and ways of working that may drastically change your job. Work schedules, ways of conducting business, and your own roles and responsibilities may be altered from what you knew before or were comfortable with. The extent of your inclination to resist the changes and maintain your former work roles may indicate which force you favor at the moment. Understanding which side you favor in the face of change—remaining the same (status quo) or moving ahead (striving)—especially in situations like this one, may save your job.

Your definitions of success are determined, in part, by who you want to be, what you think is important, and what you think other people will accept from you. Looking improperly and defensively at your labels and roles juxtaposed against your definitions of success sometimes marks the beginning of a process of fluctuation and instability that justifiably can make you feel uneasy. But once the Gordian knot of contradictory self-identification is loosened, you can realize that the process of growing is aided by change and challenge. You must be aware, however, that success and failure can feel the same, particularly during periods of transition.

As discussed earlier, everyone traverses life with an internalized reference group. This reference group acts like a Greek chorus actively kibitzing from offstage. Its basic message is always "Don't leave us!" But the embattled individual most often hears "Danger! You can't afford to go forward!" This is the song of the status quo.

The internal sum of reference group and contradictory labeling pressures interact with external reality to determine what your compromised (rather than idealized) criteria for success are. They also determine your beliefs about whether or not and under what circumstance other people will accept you.

> ARE YOUR INTERNAL FORCES FIGHTING AGAINST ONE ANOTHER? DO YOU DESIRE TO CHANGE AND DESIRE TO REMAIN THE SAME SIMULTANEOUSLY? IF SO, WHAT ARE YOU DOING ABOUT IT?

Let's look at an example of someone who is struggling to strive, and needs to learn the lesson we're all working on right now: how to strive with a purpose.

Savannah Never Smiles

Savannah H. is a senior vice president in a large Fortune 500 organization. Reared in a working-class family with parents who received little college education, Savannah decided that she was not going to live her life imprisoned by her humble and limited origins. After graduating on scholarship from an Ivy League school, she achieves success after success, finding fulfillment in making more of herself than her parents were ever able to do.

But despite her successes, Savannah, by our definition, is not *striving*. Though it appears that she is on the path to striving, she is actually running from it; and it shows in how she treats others. As her career continues, Savannah begins to avoid women like herself who are trying to make the same jump she did. She feels that to run after her lofty goals she has to leave behind the group of women that once defined her. Eventually, Savannah finds herself completely at odds with other women.

Her company asks Savannah to spearhead a women's leadership group, to share her success with them and help them acquire strategies and skills for advancement. Instead of fulfilling her responsibilities, Savannah finds every possible way to avoid them until another woman volunteers to head the group in her place.

Savannah simply can't see the point of helping other women because, as she explains one day, "Many of them are not serious about learning and aren't worth my time." As a result, Savannah refuses to help any women obtain interviews or advancement within her organization.

It doesn't take long for Savannah's direct reports to notice her bias, and before long, they are questioning her ability to assess talent and even whether or not she can succeed in her own responsibilities. They eventually label Savannah as the "woman who doesn't like other women."

Unfortunately, that label is accurate. It's impossible to ignore Savannah's anger and indifference toward women whose backgrounds are similar to hers. Contrary to what the popular Oil of Olay commercial prescribes, Savannah hasn't learned to love the skin she is in.

As Savannah discovers, succeeding at work doesn't necessarily mean you're striving. Striving is different and more complex than paychecks, promotions, and recognition. Though these may be necessary accompaniments, by themselves they are insufficient. We've seen that to successfully strive, you must accept and align yourself with your authentic self. You must embrace change and enable others. Savannah isn't doing any of those things; she's merely trying to succeed. In running from her responsibility with the women's leadership group, Savannah is running from women like herself. Savannah is, in effect, running away from Savannah. Running away is never striving. Facing your challenges and embracing the success of others is striving.

Savannah never reconciled the conflicts about her own identity: gender, race, age, and so on. She bypasses these critical issues of who she is, allowing them to compose major parts of a *negative self,* which anchors her to a status quo mentality. Thus, she discriminates against women. Clearly, Savannah is not striving in a purposive manner.

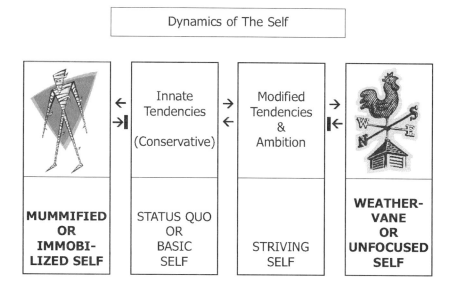

Diagram 2.1

Diagram 2.1 describes status quo and striving as forces within you. They are, in fact, constructs that help you explain the effects of your impulses. The status quo (impulse to remain the same) is heavily influenced by the negative aspects of our personality. The notion of the negative self defines a repository for negative, stereotyped, pessimistic, conflicted, and derogatory notions about the self. Herein is also contained former functioning, abandoned (not working) aspects of personality. Examples of the negative self are provided in later chapters. Likewise, the striving self is a summary of those things that lead to the tendency to strive. You will note that movement from the mummified self and from the weather vane self is blocked.

Are You Keeping Up the Status Quo? The Dangers of Going with the Flow

People trying to maintain the status quo tend to be complacent, unmotivated, and willing to mark time rather than succeed. Status quo leads to stagnation and indecision. Those of you who favor this side of the dynamic may miss critical opportunities to develop and improve, exposing yourself to a chronic feeling of anxiety and worry about life change.

> ARE YOU GOING WITH THE FLOW AND KEEPING UP WITH THE STATUS QUO, FEARFUL OF MOVING FORWARD? IF SO, HOW IS THIS IMPACTING YOUR CAREER AND LIFE? WHAT ARE YOU DOING ABOUT IT?

Status quo isn't necessarily a state of inaction, although it can be. For example, if you are more inclined to keep the status quo, you may be afraid to go against the grain, preferring to follow the movement and direction of others. Status quo is inaction, however, in terms of self-generated activity. It contains a major element of fearing to effect any change that may entail risk—such as losing your job, assuming authority or responsibility, or making a commitment to a given direction.

You may be satisfied where you are and content with remaining the same, despite indications from the environment that you need to change. Rip Van Winkle had magically falling asleep as an excuse for his inaction; typical status quo people are, for the most part, wide-awake.

When the status quo mode is powerfully fueled by fear, you may be unable to set and achieve the daily goals you need in order to learn, grow, and develop. Fear is a powerful motivator, and when the reason for it is misinterpreted, it can paralyze you and result in bad decisions. Status quo, driven by fear, can—when taken to the extreme (domination by the negative self)—lead you to an internal and even visible paralysis—which we call being *mummified*.

Take the Risk and Leave Your Mummy

Becoming mummified begins and ends with fear. On the one hand, you may be status quo, preferring to go with the flow and feeling content with who and where you are—but gradually aspects of your negative self begin to dominate the status quo mind-set. Once your fear of change takes over, you begin to avoid change at all costs, becoming virtually paralyzed in your work and life.

This fear can come from a wide variety of situations. The presence of a wild animal in your backyard, an avalanche headed in your direction, or someone creating a life-threatening event—all are causes for fear. But there are many unjustified fears.

Fear either paralyzes you or leads you to make quick decisions that are usually not well thought out. Reflect on the decision you consider to be the worst you've ever made. Was there an element of fear in your decision? Perhaps you feared disappointing someone, failing on a project, or making the wrong decision. We've all acted against good common sense because of fear more often than we'd like to admit.

Have you left your mummy? If you haven't, how is this impacting your career?

Fear can play a potent role at the office. Workers fear losing a job or losing a big client, and there are bosses out there (you may have one) who manage by fear. Has your superior ever asked, "If you had a gun to your head in this situation, what would you do?" It's become a common metaphor, but wise is the individual who answers this faulty leadership hypothetical with the response, "I'd find another job." Fear seldom works as a positive motivator. The perennially afraid are also the perennially paralyzed, whether that paralysis leads to making the wrong decision, or making no decision at all.

As earlier stated, your fear can come from a variety of experiences, situations, and people, but can often be traced back to the demands and contradictions that you find yourself confronted with. People at work, at home, and in your social surroundings are all telling you what they expect of you, often responding to your labels more than to the true you. With each expectation comes some fear of not performing up to par. If you think you've got to meet every expectation no matter what, the result may well be impaired judgment or avoidance of the situation altogether.

Today's corporate structure is especially unforgiving when it comes to dishing out fear. Companies tend to be strict and hierarchical in their organization. The appearance of an entrepreneurial spirit often masks a command-and-control structure; work environments are rarely collaborative or team-based. This type of culture stifles creativity and reduces effectiveness. Robotic obedience does not easily give way to creativity and ingenuity. It's no wonder that there are so many "walking mummies" at work!

The fear of losing your job because of subpar performance, combined with an environment that rarely allows contrary thinking, is bound to leave you indecisive and helpless. Not only do you become afraid to go against the grain, you may have little or no leeway to make decisions, even as a manager or executive with all the perks of power.

Breaking Free of the Fear

Not all of you are paralyzed by fear, or else you'd all be preprogrammed robots, incapable of making any decisions at all. No, some of you have avoided or broken free of the restraints that threatened to mummify you and have challenged the status quo. But how did you do it? And how can others do it?

First, you must pinpoint the actual risk involved in asserting yourself. The decision to act assertively requires willingness, determination, and the key ingredient that is the natural antagonist of fear—courage. Those who can get past the fear differ from those who give in to it because of a willingness to take calculated risks. It may be more than just making the decision to take the plunge that differentiates those who break free of the status quo, and those who don't.

Looking closer, the willingness to take risks is more of a mind-set than a decision, and may have come from early development and basic upbringing. If you were reared in an environment that taught you to challenge norms, to stand up for what you believe in, and not to place a lot of importance on success for the sake of success, chances are you'll be more inclined to risk job security for the sake of what you feel is right. Paradoxically, this increases your odds of rising to the top of both your career and personal life. Those employees who discreetly challenge the norm and go against the grain (although the typical work environment prescribes otherwise) may be highly valued by their organization. In order to do this, you must encounter and subdue any remnants of your negative self. And this is where the concept of striving comes in.

Harnessing the Wind and Striving Full Steam

When the winds of change come blowing, the striving self moves, but doesn't just go where the wind blows. Successful strivers are constantly looking to grow, change, and develop. They have an eye for opportunities in the present and future, but insist that these opportunities are purposive in the sense of being directional and inclusive, rather than random, opportunistic, and exclusionary.

Your inclination to strive is a generalized drive that you can direct to a specific context or environment. It combines general knowledge and specific purpose directed to a vision and a specific goal. For example, to succeed in your profession or corporate culture, you have to demonstrate specific skills, master relevant knowledge, and apply them to the vision and set of goals espoused by your organization, team, or department. Should that content change, so that your job demands things contrary to your sense of purpose, your sense of integrity and wholeness will motivate you to stop and go in another direction more in line with your values and desires. Ambition or striving without a sense of purpose or integrity tends towards a weather vane outcome.

> How's the weather around you? Do you find yourself just going where the wind blows? Is this helpful to your career?

Examples of this can be easily found in the workplace. Let's say you have worked for a company for a number of years and have formed your commitment around the principles of virtue and integrity that the company obstinately embraces. You have an inner sense of these things due to your own upbringing; thus the resultant role and label conflict resolution may have been easy. If the company's leadership changes and abandons ethical conduct, you will find yourself in conflict. They may pay lip service to creativity, personal responsibility, accountability, and ethical business practice, but if the company falls on hard times, might change and abandon ethical conduct. Questionable business decisions in the context of even more questionable ethical standards are made. At some point it affects you directly. You may be asked to compromise some of your standards "for the good of the company." Should you disagree and even rebuke others for their lack of integrity, you may be threatened with the loss your job. This is when your ethical sense should kick in and redirect the trajectory of your striving self.

Striving now is directed to succeed in a manner that doesn't require compromising your standards or directs you to leave the job altogether. On the other hand, the prospect of being unemployed is a reasonable cause to be afraid. It is a difficult path to follow. Nevertheless you may join Robert Frost and affirm that the path less traveled is the more rewarding, convinced that you will not only survive, but that you will thrive. This represents a successful reapplication of striving.

> What are your goals? What is your purpose? Where are you going in life and do you have a plan to get where you want to be?

Striving is founded on purpose. Life requires a certain degree of stability, and that stability is found in purpose; a life without purpose leads to misdirection and utter difficulty and anxiety. The fuel that defines what you do and energizes you is your purpose. It's your ultimate motivation. Your purpose should be clear in your mind.

Quite simply, striving can be your own journey to bring yourself closer to your own internal goals and purpose. And while striving is centered around your internal values, it can manifest itself in several different ways and varies, to some extent, according to context. For example, striving at work may comprise your own desires to lead a fulfilling professional life and effectively climb the corporate ladder. This might be manifested by seeking responsibility and leadership roles, promotion, advances, and increased recognition, all within an ethical framework, ultimately maintaining an inner sense of worth.

Generalized striving—born in your early upbringing, modified by personal values and ethics—becomes targeted striving in terms of your specific life experiences. Targeted striving follows the rules set by your generalized striving. In other words, you don't have one way of striving if you're gong to be a barber, and another way of striving if you're going to become a physician. Otherwise, you'd be right back to the conflict and anxiety you may have felt resolved in the first place.

Successful striving represents acting in unison with your most fundamental values and desires. It's not just the act of trying to get better at something, or accomplish some great task. It revolves around your deeply held motives: the same basic values and motives that drive your personal life dictate the specific goals or endeavors in your professional life—and every other aspect of your life in between. To truly strive, you must connect with that inner driving force.

Striving shifts contexts, but doing so is not a form of being "two-faced." While you may do one thing at work, and another thing at home, if they are both connected to the norms and values set by your generalized striving self, then you are successfully striving. Those of you who believe you can be saints at home, but sinners at work are not, by our definition, successfully striving. Any disparity in the ethical values at home and work defines a measure of unsuccessful striving; just trying to get by, or progressing along the path of the weather vane.

There is yet another important aspect of striving briefly introduced before. It is *purposive striving*, which modifies the definition of success to include the concept of wanting or needing to take others along.

How's the Weather? Avoiding the Weather Vane

While striving is your inherent mechanism for progress, achievement, and improvement, when taken to the extreme, striving can lead you right past your values and become an unquenchable and unhealthy urge. When you are striving without purpose (defining a directionless life), you become a weather vane (see Diagram 2.1).

Weather vanes align themselves with whatever way the wind is blowing and is a rudimentary indicator. Even a light puff of wind will send them spinning aimlessly.

In the same sense, a weather vane worker is tossed to and fro by the winds of change, altering direction without thought of destination, consequence, or purpose. A weather vane is enamored of passing trends and superficial goals. These people fail to identify their own inner directions. They are changing just to change, striving just for the sake of striving.

Ambition can lead to weathervane behavior. Ambition is often a wonderful motivator, but it is a double-edged sword. As you move from status quo to striving, you will undoubtedly realize personal and professional successes along the way. Yet with each success, your natural inclination will be to seek more and more success. Unless you're careful to stick with your original objectives, the goal of success for its own sake will overcome your original purpose and become your sole desire. To use a computer analogy, too much ambition and success can form an endless loop that sends the computer off into useless and infinite calculations.

> WHEN OPPORTUNITY KNOCKS IT MAY BE NECESSARY TO ASK YOURSELF, "DOES THIS RESONATE WITH MY IDEAS OF MYSELF AND MY REASON FOR BEING?"

Ethically Speaking

Once you get to the point of striving, you should be fully aware of your own values, and have become in tune with your inner core purpose and self. At this point, you may be thinking, *Why should ethics and integrity matter? It's a dog-eat dog-world.*

Moral relativity and situational ethics in the corridors of power, in corporate America and elsewhere, have eroded traditional ideas of integrity and ethical behavior. This, in turn, has contributed to a sense of insecurity and anxiety that is all too pervasive today. The place of ethical concerns in corporate America is a continuing hot-button issue.

With the unrest and instability that follow disclosure of shady dealings, it's vital to return to doing business with integrity and with regard for time-honored values. For one thing, doing business unethically carries the risk of being caught—a source of justifiable anxiety and fear, with personal and professional repercussions. The great Greek philosopher Socrates once explained that there are two competing internal forces that create who you are. Like inner voices, you either hear the call to compromise your standards or to take the moral high ground and live with integrity. According to Socrates, it's a zero-sum game: you follow the one side at the expense of the other.

A modern day example of the importance of listening to the right voice is the popular television show *Survivor*. Each season brings new castaways, new adventures, and a new sole survivor. Every season revolves around the question of who will compromise his integrity (usually represented as promises to or alliances with fellow tribe members) to get ahead. The end result is always the same: those who have chosen integrity, whether they win or lose, leave the game with a stronger sense of accomplishment, accompanied by a stronger sense of self-confidence. Those who cut corners and burn bridges do so at the expense of their own integrity, and have to face much more than the wrath of tribal council once the game has been played—though occasionally the hypocrites do walk away with a lot of cash!

HAVE YOU EVER BEEN PUT IN A SITUATION AT WORK WHERE YOU WERE ASKED TO COMPROMISE YOUR ETHICS? HOW DID YOU REACT? WHAT WAS YOUR ANSWER?

The goal of *Survivor* is to win the money. The ethical and moral lesson is secondary. In the face of this, it is surprising that losers experience a heightened sense of self when they have acted with integrity. It is easier to win at work if you cheat, but getting caught and/or feeling cheap and dishonest is too high a price to pay. Taking the high road may be the traditional way of doing business, but it's also the one that is most rewarding. Game theory teaches that games are not harmed (and may in fact be improved) by a certain amount of cheating. However, those games are destroyed when the cheating is excessive. How much is excessive? It appears to vary with the game and the number of participants, but having ten percent of cheaters will destroy most games.

Some may rationalize compromising ethics at work because everybody else is doing it. "If I don't look out for me, who will?" Others claim that such behavior is for the benefit of their family or others for whom they're responsible.

Perhaps you have learned to cut corners at the expense of your colleagues and peers and your own personal standards as well. You have convinced yourself that others must sacrifice for your benefit. You may get to the top of your company's executive team thanks to devious, unethical ways. The problem is it's hard to turn off the devious and unethical dealing. Sooner or later, many find themselves in trouble. We're not recommending that you hold the moral high ground for the sake of morality. But we believe that there's an unmistakable correlation between upholding high standards of morality and success in life.

They're Alive in You!

The forces of status quo and striving are alive in you: the balance between the two determines how you navigate the seas of stress and change. You may feel comfortable with who and where you are, and feel no need to alter your course—that is, if you want to go anywhere at all! The status quo resists change, while your striving side deals with the world as the world presents itself, giving you a vision of what's wrong, sometimes producing an uncomfortable feeling, and inviting you to catch up with the world in a healthy manner. The impetus to strive invites you to do something about that feeling of discomfort, and with the help of emotional intelligence, indicates a course of action. Whatever you do, don't ignore that uncomfortable feeling. Otherwise you're defeating yourself.

Your response to the comfort (or discomfort) you feel in how you see and describe yourself determines where you are on the status quo–to-striving spectrum. It's the difference between putting forth effort in your personal life and in the workplace (striving), and just getting by with the least amount of improvement or change while you fly beneath the radar unnoticed and unmotivated to improve (status quo). Two primary markers along the way are ambition and productivity. If you can see those two forces working actively in your life, then you are increasingly closer to the goal of being empowered.

―――◆―――

ARE YOU KEEPING UP WITH THE *STATUS QUO* OR *STRIVING*? WHAT KIND OF MEASURING STICK DID YOU USE TO DETERMINE THAT? WHAT TRAITS, CHARACTERISTICS, OR ACTIONS DO YOU FEEL INDICATE THAT YOU ARE ONE WAY OR THE OTHER?

―――◆―――

Beyond the Status Quo: The Proof of the Pudding

In a nutshell, what we've learned so far is this: to succeed in work and in life you have to:

1) discover who you are, 2) discover who others think you are and resolve the contradictions between the two perspectives, and 3) embrace change and take appropriate risks.

While life is certainly not a strictly linear progression, you must pass through each one of these steps in order to strive and reach your potential. Whether you are status quo or striving can change from day to day, and you can travel back and forth between the two. If you are mummified or behave like a weather vane, movement for you back and forth is going to be difficult.

Now that you've seen how to get beyond your fear of change and purposively strive toward worthy goals and opportunities based on who you are inside, it's time to look at how to make the most of those opportunities.

Action Items

- Identify two things that need to be changed; one at home and one at work.
- Identify who must to go along with you in order to enable that change.

Chapter 4: RoundING up THE Allies

In the middle of difficulty lies opportunity.

—Albert Einstein, physicist (1879–1955)

Step Four: Get Comfortable
IDENTIFY A CONTEXT IN WHICH YOU CAN STRIVE (EVEN IF IT'S THEORETICAL), AND FIND YOUR RIGHTFUL PLACE IN YOUR ORGANIZATION.

The next step to unlocking Your Personal Power-Up begins with understanding the corporate culture of your workplace and how you fit into it. Every office environment has its own distinctive personality. Once you know what that personality is, you can choose to conform to it in order to enjoy the accompanying rewards—status, recognition, acceptance, financial gain—or you can decide to embrace change and march to the beat of your own personal drummer somewhere else. Part of the process is to identify allies at the office who can advise, support, and encourage you along the way. Once you and your work context are in accord, there are steps you can take to help keep it that way, and other steps to consider if that isn't possible. The ultimate objective is a satisfying and rewarding career where you can succeed and still be yourself.

Identifying and Preserving the Possibility of Change
Both men and women have special problems in terms of embracing new and emerging opportunities. It would be convenient to focus entirely on the negative self as causing these problems but most of the problems that people (particularly women) have in taking advantage of emerging opportunities have to do with internalized labels, which fit approved societal definitions but sharply limit aspiration and accomplishment. It is important for both men and women who wish to move forward in their careers and personal lives to plan strategically.

There are issues of special concern to both men and women in accepting new opportunities and coexisting in the workplace. One of these is the issue of alliances, whether or not they can be formed, and how far they can be stretched. Men, as much as women, need to know whom to trust and for what they can be trusted. Men and women of color need to be particularly cognizant of the extendibility and trustworthiness of the alliances formed. This involves going beyond a friendly exchange in the environment of a bar, for example, and requires observation of the way people speak, as well as of their attitudes toward others.

Persons who are intolerant of others may turn out to be intolerant of you in predictable but emotionally unanticipated ways. A deeper level of assessment requires knowing who can be trusted in unpredictable circumstances. The ability to do so is an illustration of a skill called social intelligence.

Intelligence has many facets. You are familiar with cognitive intelligence (perception and recognition) and you have been introduced to the concept of emotional intelligence, which we consider the anchor of all the other intelligences. Social intelligence is the ability to know where you are in relation to others, if you do or do not fit in with a group (and why), and the ability to make the necessary adjustments in behavior if cooperation is a desirable goal. Again, this type of analysis is not conducive to the brief, superficial exchange of information made over drinks at a bar. Knowing what you can count on from other people in various situations takes time.

As the 21st century evolves, management ranks that are traditional and hierarchical in structure (and associated solely with male dominance) may be diminishing as more higher-level management positions are being occupied by women. Organizations and leaders who wish to be forward thinking know that in a global competitive environment, long-term sustained success is more likely to be associated with a genderless management structure. This is largely because of the changing world demographics.

What does this mean to you? One way that you can identify and preserve the possibility of change is to adopt a neutral style that blends masculine and feminine behaviors, and thus leads to better communications with colleagues, peers, managers, executives, and leaders.

Organizational structures are, by and large, constructs of male leadership styles—which have been characterized as highly political, hierarchical, competitive, and oriented toward command-and-control modes of operation. But women are given credit for possessing a more collaborative and circular leadership style, and those who have attained corporate leadership may feel a special responsibility to influence and change the corporate structure. They have to find like-minded people to fashion the alliances that can bring these changes about.

Understanding the Corporate Culture and Your Frame of Reference

Being able to do your job well is only part of what it takes to succeed at work. You also have to fit in with your coworkers and with the corporate culture. This "fit factor" is increasingly important these days in determining whether to hire or promote someone. Some aspects of the culture are obvious, such as dress codes and office hours; others are far less obvious, including decision making, risk-taking attitudes, behavior towards colleagues, and management style.

During the Super Bowl season of 2004, a TV commercial for Reebok featured Terry Tate, "The Office Linebacker," supposedly hired by the shoe company to improve productivity. In the skit, he was so successful at this that the fictitious Reebok boss said ten more people like Terry should be hired. How was Terry achieving his goal? By chasing employees down the hall and tackling anyone who looked like a slacker. This is a funny example of a rather somber situation: a culture of fear in the workplace that scares workers into performing.

> ARE YOU FORCING YOURSELF TO FIT WITHIN YOUR ORGANIZATION'S CULTURE AND NAVIGATE ITS POLITICAL CLIMATE, OR ARE YOU IN THE RIGHT PLACE?

Companies are in business to make money, not to provide you with a nice, comfortable work environment. The two are not mutually exclusive, but few corporations dedicate the time and resources required to run an open, friendly workplace. This means that in most situations, your level of contentment on the job is up to you. To establish a suitable context for yourself, you have to understand first the Where, What, Why and then the Who and How.

The Where, What, Why

Are you and your job a good fit? Looking at where you are, what the corporate culture is, and why it's the way it is, are you in the right place? At this point, if your answer is an immediate and confident no, it's time to plan your exit strategy, which we'll talk more about later. If your answer is a qualified yes—that is, you do think you can be comfortable where you are—you may be able to make this the job of your dreams with some adjustment and strategic planning.

Corporate culture manifests itself in every aspect of a business. You may understand and embrace some of it right away, but to understand it fully, you have to look more carefully, dig deeper, and tap into a network of trusted colleagues. You'll get the best and most balanced perspective by talking with a range of people, including peers, supervisors, and lower level personnel. Look at the company Web site too. All this investigating will help you bring specific themes into focus.

Even if you've been in your job a while, don't assume there's nothing more you can learn. Just being a long-term employee doesn't necessarily mean that you understand or accept your company culture. It's never too late to learn more, and this knowledge can be a very helpful tool for moving forward in your career. Corporate culture means different things to different people and is highly subjective. Remember that fact when reviewing your organization's guiding values, its communication with you, how it involves you in its business, the rewards and behaviors of management styles, executive management accessibility, and attitudes relating to risks and failure. Remember also that culture is a blueprint of basic assumptions that are constantly changing based on shifting personal relationships, business conditions, perceptions of truth and reality, and the unpredictable state of human nature in general.

As you gather information, glean the facts about your company's history from both a public and private perspective. Immerse yourself in your organization's brand by digging for an understanding of its image and whether it's aligned with how that image is perceived in the marketplace. Conduct research about key initiatives and achieved results. Who is your leadership team and what are their priorities, both short- and long-term? Learn about your leader and his or her behavior. What is acceptable, what is forbidden, and why is it this way? Study to determine both the implicit and explicit rules and norms. How does your organization define success? How does its decision-making process work? What is its financial language? The goal here is for you to add value to your worth as a member of the team by developing superior knowledge to go along with your abilities.

Let's get back to the Reebok commercial. Some of the employees were calmly walking around or having meetings in the conference room, while others were shaking in their boots or running for their lives. The calm ones were personally in sync with the corporate culture and thus a good fit in their jobs. The jury was still out on the others. Either they hadn't yet bought into the corporate culture or they weren't a good fit after all. You've got to determine which category you're part of and proceed accordingly. The higher you climb on the corporate ladder, the more challenging it is to be (or remain) a good cultural fit regardless of your job performance. Working in an unsuitable, ill-fitting organizational culture is likely to be a big hindrance to your career at any level. And since work takes up so much of the day, a cultural mismatch on the job can be a big hindrance to life in general.

Some organizations have a strong idea of their own corporate culture. In 1957, Bill Hewlett and David Packard, cofounders of Hewlett-Packard Corporation, set out to protect and preserve their company's culture in a book titled *The HP Way*. The two clearly stated their cultural intent, underscoring their belief in the importance of respecting others, establishing a sense of community, and valuing hard work. New employees received a copy of the book and so knew exactly what kind of company they had decided to join. Since then, many organizations have set out to sum up their values and goals in writing. These may be admirable, but often they say more about a company's aspirations and less about what the culture is really like.

The Who and How

If your look at the corporate culture convinces you that you could be happy in your job, start seeking out allies who can help you take the next strategic steps forward in your career.

I asked my research participants this question: *How did you receive your position within your organization and what do you believe contributed to your being hired?* Seventeen percent of men said that fitting within the corporate culture was important in their being hired. For women however, the rate was 40 percent. Here are some comments from the research demonstrating the importance of not only understanding the organizational culture and its political climate, but also knowing how to align yourself with the right people.

- Executive director of national conferences, male, age 40

  Knowing my organization, and the industry, and keeping abreast of current trends helped me speak intelligently about how I could help improve the organization's bottom line. In order to do so, I read pertinent journals, books, newspapers, etc. . . . It's not about what you know, it's about who you know, your ability to understand the politics and culture of an organization, aligning yourself with that particular culture, and relaying your skill set to the right senior executives. Finally, the key to receiving recommendations and ultimately promotions and/or job offers is by being proactive rather than reactive.

- Senior engineer, male, age 45

    The senior VP interviewed people who worked for and with me along with other senior managers. He evaluated my experience, depth of understanding in my discipline, my ability to work across organizational boundaries, ability to facilitate groups of people to accomplish objectives, and bring organizational skills into a line operation.

- Comptroller, male, age 42

    Someone I knew within the organization, the senior VP, recommended me for the position.

- Regional VP, male, age 58

    [I was] being mentored by a high level person in the organization who was a white male. Having access to influential, powerful people. He taught me the ropes, helped me understand the politics of the organization, and helped me become an expert in my field.

- Program manager, female, age 38

    Relationships with senior executives within the organization helped me obtain an interview and ultimately the position. Experience also helped.

- Executive director of human resources, female, age 52

    Qualifications, experience, and by articulating my alignment with the organization's culture and philosophy. The hiring manager was peripheral to the decision. More important were the opinions of the people who had held the position before and moved to other opportunities within the organization. Building relationships with the right people and communicating strongly. Being a leader and a trailblazer.

- CEO, female, age 49

    Informal networks of people I knew. Being friends with

> *senior executives in other large organizations who opened the doors to my being interviewed for the position. Skills, experience, background, and outgoing personality contributed to my being hired. Being frank, and up-front. I had relationships with people who could help the organization. Acknowledging my weaknesses and articulated them as strengths."*

- Senior engineer, female, age 48

  > *Being aligned with the CEO and having strong values that align with the organizational culture.*

Participants were also asked, *What do you believe is most important or key to your advancement within your organization and why?* Men, at a rate of 41 percent, said that fitting within the corporate culture helped them advance, while 60 percent of women said so. Here are some examples of answers received.

- Sales manager, male, age 40

  > *Show and prove when the opportunity was present. Create the opportunity when it is not present, and make yourself useful to all important powerful senior personnel.*

- Project manager, male, age 43

  > *Proven track record in my field. Having an entrepreneurial mind-set and skill set. Thinking and acting like the powers that be by mirroring their behavior.*

- Executive director, male, age 40

  > *Aligning with the "right" staff because they are influential and can assist in the advancement process. Fitting in with the corporate culture, and having critical projects that are highly visible along with doing your best job and doing it better than anyone else.*

- Executive director, male, age 49

  > *Building relationships with key individuals within the*

company and working collaboratively with others.

- Director of finance, male, age 45

    My ability to deal with the political climate and culture within my organization has also helped me achieve my goals, and having access to powerful people has helped me advance as well.

- Public relations manager, female, age 42

    The most important key to advancement for me was the ability to understand and play politics. In my organization what you know is certainly a deciding factor in keeping your job; however "how" you know and who you know certainly prevents folks from attacking you.

There's a consistent pattern here. Regardless of their job titles, ages, or other variables, almost every one of these research participants talk about the value of a key person, powerful executive, senior management, or other individual or group that helped him or her succeed on the job. Trusted and capable allies are an indispensable component of a satisfying career. They help you know your company better, and they help you to know yourself.

Flexing Your Muscles: Finding Your Rightful Place

So you've learned about your organization's culture, and you've decided that this is the place for you. Perhaps you've been employed in your organization for years, or you're a newcomer who has thought about quitting but you're not quite ready to leave just yet. For example, you may not like your manager, but you get along well with your peers and coworkers, and you love your organization's mission statement and commitment to its employees.

HAVE YOU IDENTIFIED A CONTEXT (EVEN IF IT'S THEORETICAL) IN YOUR ORGANIZATION AND ARE YOU THRIVING? HAVE YOU FOUND YOUR RIGHTFUL PLACE?

You may not like the bureaucratic or cliquish climate, but you enjoy flextime. You don't feel appreciated by other divisions but you're recognized and rewarded for your loyalty and hard work by your department head. There is a way for you to strive within your workplace by identifying a context (even if it's theoretical), and finding your rightful place within your organization.

By *context* we mean the various interrelated conditions of your work environment. Identifying and determining where your rightful place is within your organization takes time, but you can do it through a combination of self-efficacy, perseverance, intrapersonal empowerment, and leadership skills.

Self-Efficacy

Self-efficacy is the confidence in your own ability to carry out a specific behavior, which relates to your internal resources or motivation. Have you ever been in a situation at work where you've said, "I can't handle this situation because my boss is always on my back, and it's not going to get any better"? Have you been at your wits' end, not knowing which way to turn? Having confidence in your ability—having self-efficacy—lets you approach a task determined to do well because it's important to you. Self-efficacy produces optimism over pessimism and an ability to overcome challenging encounters. It gives you the versatility to adapt to change. Your level of self-efficacy affects your motivation level; when the level is high, you often choose to perform more challenging tasks. You tend to set higher goals for yourself and tend to stick to them. Once you take action, you're more invested and more persistent. When you face one of life's inevitable setbacks, you stay committed to your goals and recover quickly.

The Canadian psychologist Albert Bandura writes,

> *We find that people's beliefs about their efficacy affect the sorts of choices they make in very significant ways. In particular, it affects their levels of motivation and perseverance in the face of obstacles. Most success requires persistent effort, so low self-efficacy becomes a self-limiting process. In order to succeed, people need a sense of self-efficacy, strung together with resilience to meet the inevitable obstacles and inequities of life.*[1]

Perseverance

Perseverance is determined persistence and commitment to eventual success, regardless of the impediments. Self-efficacy and perseverance can go hand in hand. And while the two of them can't guarantee success, failure is far more probable without them.

Success means different things to different people, and one of our objectives is to help you figure out what it means to you. Will marrying a rich spouse bring you success? Maybe you think luck brings success, or that winning the lottery is the key. How do you define success in the workplace for you company, your employees or colleagues, and for yourself? What leads to individual and collective success in your organization? Perhaps many people have told you it takes skill and a "can do" attitude.

HOW WOULD YOU RATE YOUR SELF-EFFICACY AND PERSE-
VERANCE AND INTRAPERSONAL EMPOWERMENT ON A SCALE
OF ONE TO TEN? ARE YOU SATISFIED WITH YOUR SCORE OR
DO YOU NEED MORE PRACTICE?

Although both are very important in moving you forward in your career, one common thread that runs through the fabric of achievement and success in the workplace is perseverance. If you're chasing a successful career, perseverance is chasing you and vice versa.

The way to increase your levels of self-efficacy and perseverance is to put them into practice. Perhaps you've heard a coworker say, "I just don't have the strength or the willpower to tackle this problem." In essence, what he's saying is he doesn't have a passion or a purpose that keeps him motivated—or he hasn't learned how to persevere. If you've had these feelings yourself, don't fret—because increasing your levels of self-efficacy and perseverance can be learned by putting both into practice. It seems like simple, self-evident advice, but it works. As the great movie and Broadway star Julie Andrews explained it, "Perseverance is failing nineteen times and succeeding on the twentieth." If you have encountered barriers day after day yet decided to go the distance anyway, you already have experienced self-efficacy and perseverance. On the other hand, if you seem to drift from one joyless job to the next just for the paycheck, giving into barriers and workplace challenges, you run a high risk of failure. So what if you didn't get the support you expected and deserved? At first glance you may be convinced that your lack of success is justified. A shot of self-efficacy and perseverance is in order! Self-efficacy and perseverance separate victory from frustration and the leaders from the rest of the pack.

Marie Curie was a Polish-born Parisian scientist who won the Nobel Prize twice for her research on radioactivity (which also hastened her death). As a physicist and chemist working at the boundary of scientific knowledge, she knew all about frustration and roadblocks on the job. "Life is not easy for any of us," she once said. "But what of that? We must have perseverance and above all confidence in ourselves. We must believe that we are gifted for something and that this thing must be attained.[2]

Think about this for a moment. Is there something that you'd absolutely love to have or do that you'd work your fingers to the bone and sacrifice just about anything to get? That, in a nutshell, is what perseverance is all about. Why do you persevere? Is it for a dream vacation? A new house? A fantastic shopping spree? Is it to get that promotion you've been knocking yourself out for? You persevere in the quest of a goal. You persevere because you desire a certain achievement. You persevere out of ingrained habit that is part of your character, and you persevere through practice. To some it's second nature, like breathing.

Those of you who do not persevere feel that the "something" (goal, task, or thing) isn't enough to motivate or drive you. In other words, you're just not that into it! Another reason you do not persevere is because you haven't learned or practiced perseverance. If you've been lucky enough to have never faced barriers, stumbling blocks, or challenges, you've never had the opportunity to learn or practice perseverance. And some people just seem to be born with natural ability, drive, and persistence that others have to work hard at developing.

Think about how many times as a child you fell and scraped your knee or bumped your head in the playground. Did your parents, teachers, or whoever happened to be standing by encourage you to pick yourself up and dust yourself off, or did they rush to your side and baby you? If you picked yourself up, you practiced self-efficacy and perseverance. If you waited for somebody else to pull you to your feet instead, you didn't have the opportunity to learn or practice the development of these skills.

THINK ABOUT YOUR SCRAPED KNEE WHEN YOU WERE A CHILD. DID YOU GIVE UP AND GIVE IN, OR DID YOU JUMP UP AND START OVER AGAIN? HOW DO YOU REACT IN YOUR WORKPLACE WHEN YOU FACE CHALLENGING TIMES?

There is no magic potion that will help you develop self-efficacy and perseverance. But by employing a little introspection and getting to know your values, what's important to you (including interests), what motivates you, and what demotivates you, you will be able to learn how to increase your level of self-efficacy and perseverance. You also have to practice. By employing both self-efficacy and perseverance, which is hard work and not for the faint of heart, you will develop through experiencing your ability to overcome challenges, barriers, and difficult tasks.

WHAT MOTIVATES YOU TO HAVE A HIGH SELF-EFFICACY LEVEL AND PERSEVERANCE? WHAT CAUSES YOU TO BE STAGNANT?

Unfortunately, you can't learn how to improve simply by reading a book (even this one!). You will develop these hands-on skills through daily effort.

To some people self-efficacy and perseverance are like garlic to a vampire. But the unavoidable truth is that you've got to have them to succeed in the workplace. If you've lasted in your organization for any length of time, you already know that self-efficacy and perseverance are essential not only to retaining employment, but upward mobility in your career.

If you're an executive, leader, or mentor, create an environment that fosters self-efficacy and perseverance. Do that by encouraging your employees, coworkers, peers, and subordinates to face difficulty head-on. Don't accept excuses for not enduring a challenging task. Always keep in mind that perseverance is fueled just as much by failure as it is by success. Learn to hold yourself accountable for your own self-efficacy and perseverance through celebrating your successes and acknowledging failures; practice patience, encouragement, and push yourself toward a high standard of performance and productivity in your career and life.

As the great American women's soccer star Mia Hamm says, "No one gets an ironclad guarantee of success. Certainly, factors like opportunity, luck, and timing are important. But the backbone of success is usually found in old-fashioned, basic concepts like hard work, determination, good planning, and perseverance.[3]

Intrapersonal Empowerment

Intrapersonal empowerment and interpersonal skills are just as important as self-efficacy and perseverance. Intrapersonal empowerment is a psychological term for mental or cognitive empowerment, a process that helps you gain control over your life. This process is important because it serves as a mediator between your behavior and your social structure. Business management researchers and business practitioners all identify empowerment as a key challenge for contemporary organizations as they move from the traditional hierarchical structure to a more participative, lateral system. Empowerment takes on many different meanings in different situations. It is important to note here that your overall experience of empowerment in your workplace includes having self-determination or perseverance, competence, meaning, and an impact on your environment.

Interpersonal Skills

Interpersonal skills help you work in harmony with others and work more efficiently in teams. These are skills such as: taking the initiative to address potential problems; freely considering various opinions; understanding and appreciating people who are different from you; listening effectively; knowing when and to ask questions; giving and receiving criticism; and expressing appreciation. Employers love employees who understand team and group processes, have good conduct, and move from acceptance of self to acceptance of others. Such skills allow you to respond effectively to and resolve conflict, approach a task assertively, and evaluate and accept workplace responsibilities. Good interpersonal skills yield better communication, creativity, and productivity. It all boils down to the very unscientific concepts of being agreeable, getting along with others in the organization, a willingness to listen and learn, and a willingness to change something you're doing if you see it can be done better. Do that consistently, and you'll significantly improve your value to the company.

Will the Leader Please Stand Up?

As you continue to explore and refine your place in the corporate culture and consider the skills that will help you most, consider this: are you a leader or a manager? It's imperative that along with everything else, you also develop your leadership skills.

———⋄———

ARE YOU A LEADER OR A MANAGER? HOW DO YOU KNOW?

———⋄———

We'll explore the components of leadership in more detail a little later, but let us take a minute here to note both the importance and the distinctiveness of leaders in the process of achieving success in the workplace. Having a leader as an ally will add strength and credibility to your base of support; being a leader yourself generally yields more latitude in decision making, which means you have more control over your workplace environment and may be able to help others with their work context as well.

Leaders are as different from managers as personality types, and so are their roles. As a leader, you complete specific tasks to create a future vision and set a direction for the organization, focus on organizational alignment, and gain commitment from the individual, team, group, and organization for moving in a specific direction. As a manager, you handle other important tasks such as goal setting, metrics creation to achieve goals, budgets, and providing work groups with new technology. You may be a better manager than leader, or vice versa. Many organizations have and appreciate good managers, but are always hoping that those good managers develop into better leaders: they're looking for people who sparkle and inspire to help them forge the future.

Becoming a leader, like other processes we've seen, combines both your work skills and your characteristics as an individual. For example, no matter what your job is, you'll be a better leader if you can communicate well across all levels to all types of people. Good communication skills help you articulate a vision clearly and to attract, build, and maintain healthy relationships to help move your career forward while taking others along with you.

How many times have you heard the word *charismatic* in a list of important leadership traits? Of course charisma is important in a leader, but there's so much more to effective leadership. Great leaders have the uncanny ability to mobilize people and contribute significantly not only to the organization's bottom line (or their own career advancement), but also to the long-term development of people and the creation of an environment that fosters sustainable growth, change, transformation, adaptability, and prosperity. Leaders, when accomplishing extraordinary tasks, tend to guide others simultaneously toward the highest point of achievement.

Rounding Up Your Allies

Earlier we looked at identifying your work context (even if it's theoretical) and finding your rightful place in your organization. Alliances play an important role in helping you optimize your operational workplace context once you've identified it. Alliances are also crucial for helping you achieve success, and you must determine how to identify them, how to maintain them, and how to maximize them. When considering your alliances, you should understand:.

1. What you can count on from other people
2. How far your alliances can be stretched
3. What you can count on from yourself

Knowing what you can count on from other people in various situations—thus whether or not they will make effective allies—takes time, as we have said. It is a wise man or woman who does not exchange confidences too early, although part of the process of getting to know another person is to share information in gradually measured amounts over time. This is essential to knowing how much is transactionable. Alliances may shift, strain, or break entirely from one situation to the next. In a nutshell, you need to choose alliances that can strategically move you and the organization forward. Issues of comfort are quite secondary and may be more the responsibility of your family and friends.

Choose your allies carefully. Persons who are intolerant of others may turn out to be intolerant of you in predictable, but emotionally unanticipated ways. Dig deep to be sure whom you can trust in unpredictable circumstances. The tool you need for this task is *social intelligence*. This extremely valuable personal characteristic is the ability to know where you are in relation to others, determine whether or not you fit into a group and why, and adjust your behavior if cooperation is your goal. You can't complete this type of analysis over drinks at the bar; it takes time, care, and patience.

What Can You Count On From Others?

It's important to recognize what kinds of alliances you need to stay on a trajectory from status quo to striving, address specific issues relating to the special concerns that men and women face in the workplace, and determine how to best leverage workplace relationships. In other words, find allies that complement who you are and what you're trying to accomplish. You need to know what to look for, what to expect, and how to identify what works best in differing workplace environments (e.g., high tech, consumer products, financial, manufacturing).

You especially need good allies in times of change. Picture yourself employed in your organization for quite awhile and working hard to get a promotion that seems, at first glance, to be an excellent opportunity. Your skill set, goals, and your organization's needs appear to be a good fit. That should all improve your chances of success, right? Maybe and maybe not. The stakes are high for new leaders.

Who might your allies be and at what levels are they employed in your organization?

Statistics show that approximately 40 percent of newly promoted employees or new management hires fail within eighteen months on the job. Why? Because they're expected to deliver right out of the starting gate. Expectations are high, and some of those expectations may contain parameters that turn out to be conflicting, hidden, or unclear. Good allies under these conditions are a priceless asset.

Perhaps you've been to Europe or Asia and purchased one of those phrase books to help you understand the language, but you just couldn't get the communication thing right. Now, picture yourself being offered a new job in a different department, or in a new organization altogether, or being managed by a new person. Do you suddenly feel as though you don't understand the language or the laws? Are you an outsider in your own home (company), where you've worked for years? Are you at an extreme disadvantage? How do you assimilate and acculturate yourself? How will you survive in that strange new land and build alliances that will help you succeed?

There are five steps to take when rounding up your allies:.

1. Develop your leadership skills.
2. Avoid being overly political.
3. Build a relationship with your potential allies.

Connect with them on a human level and determine how far your alliances can be stretched.

4. Focus on learning rather than on demonstrating your own worth.
5. Be armed with a plan when you approach your potential allies.

Determine the most important goal. Have a map of how you wish to attain that goal, and be able to articulate with clarity the kind of assistance you need from your allies. For example, if you have a concern or problem, you offer the solution. Demonstrate your critical thinking skills, appropriate risk taking, high levels of self-efficacy, perseverance, and intrapersonal empowerment.

To see whether or not you're ready to begin your search for allies, put yourself in the other person's shoes. If you approached yourself for assistance, would you help you? If the answer is yes, proceed. If the answer is no, then you have more work to do. Be realistic and understand that you're being judged by others as to whether or not you can pull your own weight. Why should others help you if they don't think you're serious about success? Others are already judging you every day and deciding whether to help you or undermine your progress if they have the chance. Plenty of coworkers would welcome the opportunity to help someone move forward in their career, but if the stakes are too great and the risks are too threatening, they may shy away from offering a helping hand for fear of associating with failure.

Remember, too, that rounding up allies involves give and take. Ask yourself what strengths and challenges you bring to the table. Are you a true leader? Are you worthy of other people taking a risk on your behalf? Answering these questions honestly will help you move ahead with the process.

ARE YOUR ALLIES INFLUENTIAL AND POWERFUL PEOPLE?
DO THEIR PASSIONS, VALUES, AND BELIEFS MIRROR YOURS?
CAN YOUR ALLIES BE STRETCHED—AND AT WHAT RISK?

What Can You Count On From Yourself?

I also identified the four strongest workplace strategies for helping find and develop the right alliances:

1. Participate in effective mentor/protégé relationships.
2. Gain clarity about how your role may change in your organization throughout your career.
3. Understand internal politics and develop your own political skills.
4. Meet key objectives.

You can further increase your chances of success by demonstrating trustworthiness, a can-do attitude, willingness to collaborate, and flexibility to match your organization's changing roles and environment. Work also to be results oriented, articulate in stating your goals, a good motivator of yourself and others, and able to have effective cross-cultural communication with departments, other managers, and senior level executives.

Jeff's Story: A Cog in the Machine

Jeff is a director of software sales and development. His story illustrates the tension between what the workplace is really like for many employees and what they need and want in a corporate environment. His experience touches on a number of ideas we've discussed to this point.

As a child, Jeff was happy, inquisitive, curious, and gravitated toward others. He was active in school, which attracted the attention and approval of his teachers. He had lots of friends, yet on the other hand he also had his share of troubles: peer pressure, peer problems, bullying, and name-calling. Overcoming these challenges motivated Jeff as he grew older; he refused to consider himself a punching bag or to take punishment from someone else because of their own insecurities. He wanted to be able to get what he desired out of life. After high school, he enlisted in the military in order to travel and get a college education. Along the way he also gained experience with the top-down, command-and-control style of military organization, and learned how to work with a team toward a common goal.

Having left the military with an engineering degree, Jeff is hired by a major corporation that creates software for the high tech industry. Over the next fifteen years, he progresses in his career at several Fortune 500 companies from software engineer to his current position as director of sales and development. As our story begins, Jeff is meeting with Wilfred, one of his sales executives, who has just turned in his letter of resignation effective immediately. Jeff doesn't want to lose Wilfred, who has an MBA and ten years of experience selling software to senior-level executives.

"Wilfred," Jeff says, "this is a complete surprise. What's happened? You mean a lot to this team and we'd sure hate to lose you."

Wilfred drums his fingers on the table and thinks for a moment. "You know I love selling and love my clients, and I'm making good money," he says at last. "But Jeff, I'm tired of the way people run things around here. I'm sick of the hierarchy; I've had it with the cutthroat competition and what-have-you-done-for-me-lately attitude. As hard as I work, I don't think anybody listens to me or appreciates me. I'm exhausted, I've had it with the authoritarian mind-set in this organization, and I think it's time to move on."

Jeff nods his head slowly as Wilfred continues. "It's not you, Jeff. You're one of the best directors I've ever had. There's nothing you could have done differently." Their meeting over, Jeff and Wilfred shake hands and part as friends.

Jeff has to admit that the corporate realm is typically a dysfunctional place. His own company follows inefficient procedures, but people in the organization and in his own department are very resistant to change.

They'd rather work around the problem than correct it.

At the end of the day, Jeff pours out his frustrations to his wife.

"Why are there are so many problems with the corporate culture? People are always playing games, dealing with rampant favoritism, tiptoeing around certain workers they wish they could avoid completely. The executive management doesn't really know what's going on but won't listen to any criticism or suggestions. They don't want to spend money to change the system, but they don't understand how badly it needs changing. They claim they have an open door policy, but if you go against the system you risk being branded as a traitor."

Jeff goes on to say there are people who have a chance to push for change, but first they have to earn the trust of the system. They have to be willing to fit in. "It reminds me of being in the military," he continues. "You have to have credibility to be accepted and offer suggestions. Otherwise, the consensus is, 'How dare you! Because I have earned the right to criticize, you must earn the right to criticize, and you will not be heard until that happens!' You've got to understand the politics and stick to both the implicit and explicit rules if you want to succeed—and there's still no guarantee."

His wife asks, "What do you have to do to earn the chance to be accepted and heard?"

Jeff sighs. "I know from experience that to be accepted you have to be making money for the company, stay in the good graces of senior executives, and stay out of the dog house. In order to survive in the corporate world you have to be likable and accepted on the team. You have to be someone who fits in—or appears to—and who doesn't buck the system."

Jeff can't fix the problems Wilfred spoke about. He's just a cog in the machine. He can only do what he can, which is be the collaborative, forwarding-thinking person he is, and try to be the best manager possible.

Frustrated though he is at his corporate context, Jeff has arrived at an important conclusion. The demanding corporate environment isn't going to change for his benefit, but there is a pathway to a satisfying and rewarding work environment for "someone who fits in." And we're almost there.

Action Items
- Identify your workplace context and find your rightful place in your organization.
- Identify your potential workplace alliances.
- Be strategic when forming and managing your relationships.

Chapter 5: Satisfaction: Creating a Workplace Context

Every second is of infinite value.

—Johann Wolfgang von Goethe, German writer (1749–1832)

Step Five: Carpe Diem
SEIZE THE DAY AND TAKE CONTROL OF YOUR LIFE BY CREATING AND CLAIMING A WORKPLACE ENVIRONMENT WHERE YOU CAN SUCCEED.

Analyzing and Understanding Your Existing Work Context

Your work environment, or context, includes both stipulated, overt conditions (company rules, who your boss is, who reports to you) and unstated, covert conditions that workers seldom talk about but that are just as real and important as the others: company tradition, taboos, politics, personal agendas, and so forth.

To survive and thrive in the workplace and take confident control of your career and your life—to *seize the day*—you have to have a strategy for dealing with both the obvious and the hidden. What other people at the office are essential to your strategy? If they become aware of your plans, will they be helpers or adversaries? You need to understand how to use your alliances to create or alter a work context to produce the best possible individual environment for your own purposive striving, working consciously and confidently towards established goals.

HOW DO YOU EVALUATE YOUR CURRENT WORK CONTEXT? HOW HAS YOUR CURRENT WORK CONTEXT BEEN TESTED AND UNDER WHAT CIRCUMSTANCES? DO YOU FEEL THAT YOUR CURRENT WORK CONTEXT IS GOOD, OR DOES IT NEED TO CHANGE?

We'd like to share a story with you now that illustrates many of the points we've been discussing in a single sweep. You'll see a troubled work context, the importance of changing it, the challenges and risks that accompany change, the key role of allies in the process, and the value of maintaining your integrity above all else. In this case, a few dedicated colleagues led the charge in transforming their corporate environment into a place where workers could excel and still be true to themselves. Confident about who they were and what was important to them in their lives and careers, they were brave enough to upset the status quo even though they couldn't know whether they would ultimately succeed or fail. The star of our story is an unlikely hero: a middle-aged senior human resource specialist named Cora.

Cora Seizes the Day

Cora works for a national car rental company, and one of her responsibilities is to conduct exit interviews with departing employees. Today she is disappointed to learn that a promising executive assistant trainee named Mary is resigning because Mary's boss, Dina, is difficult to work for.

"I love my job," Mary says, "and I could see myself working here for a long time. But I can't take Dina any more. She talks down to me like I'm a child. The criticism never stops." Mary goes on to say that Dina is bossy, aggressive, overbearing, and has a nasty attitude.

This isn't the first time Cora has had complaints about Dina, and she knows it won't be the last. As a girl, Dina was rewarded with candy and toys when she was obedient, and punished with no TV and no outside play when she disobeyed. As a senior executive assistant, the adult Dina is very familiar with the carrot-and-stick method for getting what she wants, and she's quick to use the stick. Dina herself is a quick learner and doesn't like it when new hires ask too many questions. Either they get it or they don't, and if they don't get it fast enough, they're not good enough.

Others have complained to Dina's manager, Larry, the executive director of marketing, but Larry has done nothing because he knows that his own boss, Kathy, the marketing VP, thinks Dina is doing a great job. Larry is afraid to rock his own little boat by challenging Kathy. As a result, Dina continues to terrorize her fellow workers because her tactics are reinforced by her superiors, and Larry becomes notorious as "Chicken Larry" because he won't act on the complaints. Turnover continues to climb, productivity slides, trainees come and go in a constant stream, and morale sinks lower and lower.

Convinced that this sort of trouble happens systemwide, Cora sends out a confidential survey to 3,000 employees, 45 percent of whom report that they've worked for, or are currently working, for an abusive boss!

Cora and her staff know they have to act, and begin by attending a seminar on workplace bullying. There she finds a startling array of statistics, including the fact that 71 percent of workplace bullies are managers of other people and 58 percent of bullies are women. Half of all workplace bullying is woman-on-woman, though women, at a whopping 80 percent, are far more likely to be targets than men.

Cora learns that the Healthy Workplace Act, introduced in twelve states, allows victims of workplace bullying to file lawsuits against their employers for psychological harassment. This type of harassment often results in physiological aftereffects (researchers call them *sequelae*) such as obesity, heart disease, and hypertension. Cora realizes that her organization has done nothing to address the issue of bullying, even though it's considered a form of workplace violence that affects employees' health and self-esteem. Workplace bullies, the seminar confirmed, can be productive and successful in limited roles (positions in which they have no one to bully), but in positions of power, they cause trouble. If further legislation passes, there could be a flood of lawsuits.

Cora continues her research by interviewing Theodore, a district manager who has worked for two different bullying regional district managers, Dick and Jane. Theodore is an excellent employee who is about to resign because he's sick of being embarrassed and belittled. It's further evidence to Cora that she and her company can't keep ignoring the cost in attrition, lost productivity, absenteeism, and higher health care and worker compensation expenses that bullying causes. In fact, the expense nationwide runs into the billions. Nevertheless, Cora decides not to take on Dina as yet.

Theodore's Story

Dick and Jane, who manage about 125 employees each, hold quarterly regional meetings together because they feel it will be cost-effective for the company. Theodore is outspoken and vocal, an out-of-the-box thinker whose customers adore him and whose peers respect him. His employees love him because he always goes out of his way to make sure they have the tools they need to achieve success. But during the meetings, Theodore is a constant butt of jokes from Dick and Jane.

When Dick and Jane announce a new marketing plan, Theodore has some question about it.

"It's a great idea," he volunteers, "but I feel it needs to be tweaked a little to reflect the unique challenges of our region and districts." A hush falls over the conference room as Dick and Jane exchange glances. Then, ignoring Theodore completely, Jane turns to another participant and has a short conversation before looking over at Theodore and saying,

"Sometimes people can ask the dumbest questions, can't they?"

Dick chimes in. "You're right Jane. It's amazing that some people have made it this far in the company. If I had my way, some people in this room would no longer be here." Others in the room chuckle nervously. At least *they* weren't the one being hammered by the regional bosses.

Just telling Cora the story has made Theodore jittery and unsettled. "I feel intimidated, threatened, and offended," he says at last. "Ted [another district manager] thinks they get some kind of sick thrill out of it. And there's more to it," he continues. "They're out to sabotage me. They don't return phone calls from me, don't respond to meeting requests, and ignore calls from customers in my district." Cora sees that both Dick and Jane have given him negative performance reviews, while previous managers have made glowing remarks and compliments about his performance.

"Theodore, we're going to fix this," Cora says. "Just give us some time."

Theodore agrees to hang on a while longer.

Digesting her seminar information, Cora learns that bullies are often found in highly competitive environments that tend to foster the behavior, or are in positions of power and feel a sense of entitlement, allowing them to explain away the mistreatment of others—exercising power while simultaneously feeling powerless. These folks often have their eye out for hardworking, ethical, and highly competent employees because they themselves have a frail, overinflated sense of self. Bullies feel threatened and want to protect their positions. Unfortunately, it usually works: the bullies stay and those who are being bullied leave.

Cora had the authority to deal with Dick and Jane, but she was uncertain about the cost of doing so. She had not checked her alliances for some time. She needed to reassess her environment and round up her allies before taking on the bullies. Another critical part of rounding up allies was careful discussion of the complaints with peers and superiors. No predator, unless starving, will attack a prey capable of inflicting sufficient damage to impair the predator's efficient functioning. The survival rules for business enterprise are about the same. Exercising power to win a battle isn't worth it if the result diminishes the winner's effectiveness. It would take courage, integrity, and strategic caution for Cora to do her job.

But before we move to the climax of the story, we need to take a moment to consider a component of the workplace environment that has a profound effect on our discussion. What difference would it make if Dick were Black and Theodore Caucasian? Or if the two were reversed? What if Theodore were sixty years old? What if Cora were Black (which she is)? Suddenly the joking and bullying all means something else. There have been, so to speak, three elephants in the room here: gender, age, and race. They are the perceptual lynchpins around which the most common biases—sexism, ageism, and racism—are built. These elephants have appeared all through man's history, but in the twenty-first century our business culture is finally addressing them. Cora is a middle-aged Black woman who has been challenged by each of the elephants in turn and simultaneously. For Cora to function effectively, her organization has to be serious about workplace diversity, rights, and obligations.

Thinking the matter through seriously now, Cora realizes she doesn't believe her organization has integrity, and for that reason she hasn't looked for alliances. She was afraid she couldn't find them, or that that they might only pay lip service when the going got rough. In the end, Cora decides to act out of a sense of self-respect and self-preservation, and therefore has to develop a strategy.

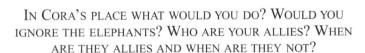

IN CORA'S PLACE WHAT WOULD YOU DO? WOULD YOU IGNORE THE ELEPHANTS? WHO ARE YOUR ALLIES? WHEN ARE THEY ALLIES AND WHEN ARE THEY NOT?

Affidavits from employees Dick and Jane have savaged show Jane is the primary offender. Dick followed suit in most instances. Cora sees this as an opportunity to shrug off one of the elephants (sexism). She files a formal complaint for harassment against Jane on behalf of the candidates, while indicating to upper management that she actually has ample evidence for a class action suit. Upper management gets the message: Jane is demoted and Dick has the fear of justice put into him. Cora tells the director of the mentoring program that the program should emphasize the hazards of the abuse of power. Seeing the advantage of her advice, the program director becomes a willing ally. Because she doesn't file a lawsuit as she could have done, Cora finds upper management on her side as well. Of course, the employees who had been slighted in various ways by Dick and Jane support her too. Cora is surrounded by allies at every level. When the next exigency arises, she'll have plenty of help in dealing with it. Now Cora is ready to deal with Dina.

Cora remained true to her sense of integrity but experienced great anxiety in the process, which came from not having a sense of who her potential allies might be. Once Cora evolved a strategy, her anxiety diminished greatly, and when she began working actively on her alliances, her anxiety virtually disappeared.

If Cora had been ten or fifteen years older, would she have been willing to take the same risk and go to the same amount of trouble? As people age, their willingness to take risks diminishes, even when they should do so to maintain personal integrity. We suggest that inability to resolve this conflict is a signal for retirement. Indeed, the elephants tend to induce this kind of response across the board because they induce fear. But gender- and race-sponsored conflict have no natural refuge in retirement. In such cases, failure to resolve the conflict calls for job change. On the heels of her victory over Jane, Cora scheduled meetings with the mentoring programs directors and instituted a "trouble anticipating" function in HR using, of all people, a fearful and penitent Dick as an advisor! Upper management, relieved at having dodged a bullet, endorsed and supported Cora's efforts. Jane, without Dick, caused no more trouble.

Cora Advises Jeff

While Cora solved her problem and transformed her workplace, you may recall we left Jeff at the end of the previous chapter wondering what he should do. He saw the whole American business system as tainted. What advice can Cora give Jeff about his situation? Let's imagine they've met and explained to each other what they do. Jeff's job makes him highly visible and accountable; Cora's success is measured in terms of employee satisfaction and reduction of conflict.

Jeff: "I struggle with my own accountability and integrity under the corporate system. Is the very structure of corporate America responsible for so much misery among employees? It reminds me of the command-and-control structure in the army. When I was a captain in the service the system seemed to work fine, and it brought great camaraderie. Now I've got the command-and-control but not the camaraderie."

Cora: "I was never in the military, but I think that in my corporation command-and-control is less of an issue. In fact, we have a lot of freedom in how we attain a given goal. For me, a middle-aged Black woman, camaraderie was never a goal, but I agree that there isn't much of it in my work scene either."

Jeff: "I feel responsible when good people leave us feeling despoiled and unappreciated. My integrity pushes me to lead in areas I feel strongly about, but the command-and-control structure blocks my leadership efforts and I end up feeling so frustrated."

Cora: "I need to exercise leadership in order to maintain a sense of personal integrity. One of the things I've done is develop a reporting network to head off trouble before it has a chance to take root. I can do this without interfering with anyone else's management responsibility, but if necessary, I will take on the organization to get the job done. I have my allies to help me, and I'd want to be sure of them before I acted."

Jeff: "At this point I'm so disgusted that I'm ready to follow some of my former associates out the door. Are you saying I shouldn't give up without 'taking on the organization?'"

Cora: "Yes. Do some homework first. Find like-minded people you can count on as allies, and decide how far those alliances will stretch."

Jeff: "How long will it take to build a network? Does it vary based on things like how well you are liked and how much money you have made or saved for the company?"

Cora: "Those things do matter, but the level of respect you have is far more important. I have learned that the sooner you start exploring and developing your network, the better things go."

Jeff: "What if you run into opposition from the onset?"

Cora: "If the opposition trumps your ability to build alliances and to form a consensus around viable issues, then it may be time to leave."

Jeff: "But if I do leave after a best effort, I intend to step right up and do it again at the next job. I'm ashamed to say that as a white male in middle management, I've been inclined to blame company concerns with diversity issues for a feeling of powerlessness rather than my own lack of leadership initiative."

Cora: "I dealt successfully with two abusive employees who had harassed and discouraged talented new recruits. Because I hadn't researched and hadn't shored up relationships, I couldn't deal with them together, although their actions were often in tandem. I was afraid to take them on together because they were a white male and female. I wasn't sure how serious my organization was and is about fairness, or, frankly, how the management feels about me as a Black female."

Jeff: "I don't blame you for being afraid. There is so much hypocrisy it is really hard to know where you stand. But you're part of HR—whose function it is to ensure diversity, safeguard employee's rights and interests. It seems to me that you can only be as effective as your department is."

Cora: "Exactly. But what I should have been doing—and what I'm doing now—is having weekly meetings with all of HR to tell them my areas of concern and, equally important, to listen to theirs. I have urged a weekly meeting with top management so they'll know how we're reading the level of employee satisfaction. My organization is so relieved to have avoided a class action suit that they're going along willingly. For the first time I'm feeling somewhat secure and not living in the shadow of the elephant in the room."

Jeff: "You don't have to hit specific productivity goals, but our division does, and we're competing with other divisions as well as among ourselves. Top management exploits this tenuous balance between competition and cooperation. My wife advises me to keep my head down and just go with the flow, but I want to *lead*. It's not like I was back in the army, but I expect my bosses to take my assessment seriously, and also my evaluation of my direct reports."

Cora: "You've got to build respect. That's a process that takes time."

Jeff: "So you're saying that *I've got to win with the company's game plan* first in order to earn their respect so they'll be willing to change their plan, including personnel recommendations."

Cora: "Yes. But I'm sure you have enough autonomy to be able to reward some of your best people, within limits. Have you made the most of that autonomy?"

Jeff: "Possibly not. But there's only so much that you can do on your own level."

Cora: "But you can still do a lot. Go to bat for them. Help them meet and exceed corporate expectations. If you win a reputation as a superb leader, that respect will enhance your influence."

Jeff: "Makes sense to me. Also, I think we can define success as more than productivity goals: it's moving the balancing point between cooperation and competition more in the direction of cooperation."

Cora: "If you've built your alliances well enough and what you stand for is clear throughout your organization, but the opposition is still overwhelming, then you really need to find a new organization and begin all over again."

Jeff and Cora have underscored the importance of purposive striving and the importance of being able to assert leadership in all areas in order to do so. Purposive striving alters the dimension of competitiveness, although competition is still in the picture. In addition to underscoring the importance of leading in some fashion, this conversation also shows the importance of maintaining a sense of integrity. To preserve integrity, you must exert leadership in whatever areas of autonomy you have. This earns you respect which, like money in the bank, you can draw upon to repeat the cycle and do more purposive striving. Once again, self-knowledge is the key to both purposive striving and the exercise of leadership.

The Risk Factor: Maintaining Your Work Context After You've Created It

Alliances can shift based on changing interpersonal and situational dynamics. As you develop and maintain your work context, it's important that you establish parameters that identify, for you, the cornerstones of your integrity (the functional, socialized self). Ask yourself:

1. Will I be able to significantly affect the environment in which I have elected to work?

2. If not, can I uncover and understand the reasons why I can't affect my work environment?
3. How much of a risk am I willing to take in order to attempt to make a change in my work environment?

There are stipulated and open conditions within every work context, but there are also unstated and covert conditions that are seldom discussed but just as binding as the stipulated set. (For example, you cannot wear argyle socks in military uniform.) If you are a manager and find the dress code unreasonable, what is the cost to you and your effectiveness in altering it? Can you sustain it or must you back down with loss of face and influence? If you cannot assert your preferences either for yourself or on behalf of others, what is the cost of suppressing your impulse to rebel? This reinvokes the notion of risk analysis. Picture yourself in a situation that you're uncertain about; for example, the senior vice president of sales has called an emergency meeting of the sales department. You and your team have exceeded your sales goal for the month (an event that's desirable). But what if those sales caused a shortage in inventory and delayed shipments (an event that's undesirable)? Because the delay in shipping creates the potential of losing orders, a possibility of risk rears its ugly head.

The possibility of any event that is undesirable and/or the possibility of damage and loss are considered to be risks. If you are the sort of person who prefers to have a low risk level, you're not alone. Most people do. And if you can keep your risk level low, you have a higher probability of realizing some form of gain such as success and profit.

It's important to continuously analyze your risks. Where do the risks lie in your work context? How significant will they be? As you are aware, no matter what type of change you experience, some risk is involved, whether it's desirable or undesirable. You can quantify (attach a price tag) and qualify the risks once you have identified where they are. Then you'll be able to determine whether or not you are willing to take the risk to maintain your operational work context.

In maintaining a work context that works for you, it's imperative that you maintain a pulse on your ethical stance; strive to maintain your morals, values, and beliefs. Additionally, continual observation, analysis, and adjustments must be made to maintain the workable context. It will not maintain itself—it depends on a series of dynamic alliances and understandings that are responsive to internal and external stressors. Although extremely difficult, it is advantageous to have a prepared strategy if one finds oneself functionally threatened.

Alliances and strategies can shift, based on changing interpersonal and situational dynamics. These shifts affect the degree to which you can effectively move from the status quo to striving. You need to understand how to utilize alliances to alter or create a work context that maximizes your purposive striving by:

1. Being aware of social networks within the organization, and how information moves through these networks.
2. Knowing how information is distributed in your organization.
3. Understanding how and to what extent collaboration is either accepted or rejected in an organization that is a hierarchical culture.

Your perception of your work context is influenced by factors at both the individual level and work group level, and it's important that you are able to evaluate those factors as you strive to maintain your operational work context.

Essential Ethics: Being a Person For All Seasons Versus Situational Ethics

A 2006 study by the American Management Association and the Human Resource Institute found that as organizations jockey for competitive advantage in the global economy, their leaders put a high value on ethics for two reasons: to protect their reputation and brand, and because it's the right thing to do. Organizational leaders and employees also recognize that there is greater pressure to behave in an ethical manner. Whether they do or not can directly affect the corporate bottom line. The study also linked ethics to some important issues such as workplace conditions, employee rights, safety, health, harassment, and discrimination.

> HAVE YOU EVER BEEN PLACED IN A POSITION WHERE YOUR ETHICS WERE CALLED INTO QUESTION? HOW DID YOU HANDLE THE SITUATION? DID YOUR DECISIONS AND/OR ACTIONS COME BACK TO BITE YOU?

Intensified globalization and competition are challenging leaders and employees to maintain a pulse on their ethical behaviors and uphold not only corporate values but their own personal values as well. And when those two sets of standards diverge, they have to choose one or the other. The old saying has never been more true: you can't serve two masters.

Let's consider a narrative that helps illustrate the big picture.

Lillian's Story: Never Compromise When It's Time to Let Go

As a girl, Lillian learned to put all she could into her work. She also learned that the good things you do will come back to you as well as the bad, so you have to be very careful about what you do and why you do it. Never exalt yourself or get intoxicated by the praise of others because in the bigger context, we're all the same. Having worked her way up to corporate vice president, Lillian has the opportunity to lecture to MBA students and share her insights. She tells them, "When you work in corporate America, it is imperative that you know who you are. Never look to others to affirm your significance as a human being. You are of great value, period. It is important that you do not let anybody else make you feel any less. Don't sell your soul to the highest bidder. Never compromise when it's time to go. You're young, vibrant, eager for success. Don't let others define what success is or create a context for you. Define that context for yourself."

Driving home from a lecture, Lillian goes over what she said that evening. *Too bad those youngsters are in for a big surprise*, she thinks. *Corporate America can be a cynical, politically charged place.* Lillian herself has two bosses, Valerie and Clifton, in two different cities, each very territorial and inclined to behavior out of line with her values. Since neither one of them hired her, neither one really likes her. The two have different leadership styles, business objectives, corporate philosophies, and work habits. It's tough for Lillian to be all things to all people. Nevertheless, Valerie and Clifton realize that Lillian knows their bosses better than they do. Therefore they see her as a threat because she's one person they can't control. Lillian has figured out how to survive in this context, but she can't sustain it in the long run. Deep down, she knows she can't continue to play corporate politics.

Lillian has seen many people do this in the workplace only to be disappointed in the long term. She has played the game, but she's had enough and feels as though it's time to let go. Now it's time for her to decide whether to build a context where she can purposively strive or let the workplace go in order to save herself.

If you were Lillian, what would you do?

Now let's meet another person who's weighing whether or not he should keep trying to get comfortable with his present employer or head off in another direction.

Paul's Principles for Success

Paul is a fifty-two-year-old director of software and hardware development for a global manufacturer; he has a master's degree in management and engineering. At his annual physical, his doctor tells him he's showing signs of stress. "I visit people in the hospital every day who don't know when to say when," the doctor observes. "They feel so defeated that their backs curve and their heads hang down like weeping willows. Tell me about what's going on with you."

Paul came to his career after growing up in a working-class family. His mother only finished the eighth grade and his dad had one year of college, but they constantly emphasized community service and education. After his parents divorced, Paul was the one who got along with both sides; in his personal and professional lives he became known as "Mr. Fix-it" or "the man in the middle." He graduated with a degree in computer technology, even though he struggled with dyslexia. He always focused on achievement and refused to let anyone outdo him.

"I've got a good track record at work," Paul says, "but I'm concerned about the future. I want to be successful—and I'm not sure I can be. To me, success is focusing on people and helping them succeed. This, in turn, is based on three principles: 1) truth and truth telling, 2) learning, and 3) leaving something behind."

Paul goes on to describe them in more detail. *Truth and truth telling* are especially important in large corporate settings. Can you do what you say you're going to do when you say you're going to do it? Meet your commitment to everyone, eliminate deceptive thinking and doing. Successful people are always *learning*. They like the challenge of learning new things, and they learn to apply their knowledge quickly to add value. In regards to *leaving something behind*, Paul believes people don't want you around if you're not going to help them work smarter, so he tries to add something to the mix. These principles define the meaning of success for Paul.

"I try to collaborate with everybody, but our culture is so competitive that people don't trust each other, "Paul says. "I've never been afraid of competition. The problem is that it gets cutthroat. The attitude is 'Get it any way you can, because this is war!' To the eighty people I manage, that means it's all right to be dishonest, deceptive, and take credit for other people's work. It really is like a war zone, where some employees try to make others crash and burn, so they'll look good by comparison.

"But I really make sure that the definition of success is at the forefront of my conversations with my team, colleagues, and superiors. I allow people who are different and who other managers don't want to join my team. Now I embrace people who have different ideas.

"When I first took over the international IT group, I went to training in order to deal with different cultures. When my international team came to the United States for team building, we got to know one another, and began to align our thinking. The leader I chose for the team has never managed, wears a beard and t-shirts, and literally looks like a hippie. However, he is really smart and knows how to relate to people. I'm a collaborative thinker whose philosophy is less about managing day to day, and more about building a community. Relationships are more important than technology. I'm committed to my team. The team really likes this because they connect to one another and the company's goals.

"I take people that others didn't want. For example, I hire out-of-the-box thinkers, some who are disciplined and some who aren't. In addition to my hippie team leader, and I also hired a woman who doesn't follow orders well—she's not subservient. She became one of my best friends and allies, and is now a senior vice president. If I had someone who worked against the good of the whole, I'd try to coach him, give him time to develop, and if he didn't grow, I'd move him out.

"What really bothers me now is that I've run across people in my organization who are deceptive and not forthcoming. Dad reared us to think facts were important," Paul continues. "I'm a matter-of-fact person and I've never been cliquish, but around here the environment is cliquish and not trusting. Even though I'm successful, I feel like I just don't fit in this environment.

"I just can't accept the context of my work environment. The lack of trust is very disappointing; it makes me feel disrespected and a failure. I've been successful throughout my career, but now I feel as though I'm just earning a paycheck because I'm in an operational context in the work environment where I can't thrive and be whole. Senior executives have encouraged me to stay and milk it, but I can't do that because I respect myself. I can't sit here, pretend that it's okay, and go along with the program."

Although Paul has established many workplace alliances, he understands that there is just so much that people will and can do for you without jeopardizing themselves. Like Lillian, he has to make a decision whether or not he will stay, and try to create a context in his work environment that is operational for him, or accept the context that is already operational.

Individuality in the Corporate World

Raising your awareness of the corporate identity as it relates to your own identity is an important part of keeping your focus and your integrity. The degree of success you'll have in maintaining your individuality and remaining successful both personally and professionally over time depends to a great degree on your ability to structure your operational work context. By now we hope it's clear that there are advantages as well as risks to buying into a corporate identity.

> WHAT TYPE OF CORPORATE IDENTITY IS EVIDENT IN YOUR ORGANIZATION? IS THE CULTURE ONE OF HIERARCHY, COMMAND-AND-CONTROL? IS IT STRICTLY AUTHORITARIAN IN THEORY AND PRACTICE?

By highlighting the corporate identification and de-emphasizing your own, you risk returning to the label box with all its inflexibility and potential difficulties. A confident sense of self-knowledge minimizes these risks: even as you dig in and become part of the corporate personality, knowing who you are inside preserves your individuality.

Once you've established your individual identity in the corporate world, you have to work to hold onto it. As you and your job both change over time, and as the company and your colleagues undergo changes of their own, you'll discover that what preserved your individuality at one point won't work forever. When you first landed your job, no matter where it was on the corporate ladder, it was the necessary initial step in beginning a career path: you've got to start somewhere. Then or later you may have thought you had a handle on the brass ring of achievement and success. But that ring is slippery and you have to keep changing your grip to hold on.

Is it possible to grasp the brass ring in different ways—in other words, can you keep adjusting to changes in the workplace and still maintain your own identity? Once you've gotten a tight grip, you've still got to be flexible and ready to adjust your hold if conditions require it. Knowing your core self is like hanging onto that ring. Conditions change and you adjust accordingly, but without losing your understanding of who you are. It's risky to modify that core to keep your hold, and doing so can be disastrous. Having said that, however, it's also true that suppressing your individual identity is not necessarily catastrophic. Many have done so (not without pain) and have become effective cogs in a machine. The ideal goal is for you to maximize individuality and creativity in a work setting that permits and encourages it. Nonetheless, there are times as you grow, and you and your company both change, that you may have to give up the corporate identity where you are and look for other career opportunities in order to remain true to yourself. Your cog may no longer fit, so to move ahead you have to connect with your inner self in another setting.

The corporate identity is one of the most powerful cultural forces in the world today. You can instantly think of a list of company names, slogans, type treatments, logos, color schemes, and symbols. Big companies spend billions of dollars to make sure you remember them with the hope that you'll buy their products. They generate and promote a symbol or image that paints a carefully crafted picture of the company behind it. For example, when you see two golden arches paired with the words I'm lovin' it, McDonald's immediately comes to mind; you can almost taste those fries. You immediately recognize Coke's distinctive script logo. When you see the Nike® swoosh you can just picture yourself running in those shoes, or beating Tiger Woods at golf. There's Google, Mickey Mouse, Michael Jackson's glittery white glove, and the Olympic rings—all effective images, symbols, and color schemes known around the world.

Perhaps you work for a highly recognizable company with a very strong corporate identity. But corporate identities and brands are ever changing in today's competitive and fast-paced economy. Just as companies need to evolve to realize long-term survival, so do you as an individual employee. It's important that you maintain your individuality and creativity while continuing to evolve.

Faced with such a powerful corporate image and personality, how can you be a part of such an organization and still hold onto your own inner self? How do you find an operational context in a corporate minefield like Lillian and Paul had to deal with—or in *any* corporate environment? The most reliable way is to assert your leadership skills.

The Characteristics of a Strategic Leader

Whatever the job, all leaders have special characteristics that equip them for their responsibilities. First and foremost, strategic leaders are strategic thinkers. Strategic leaders are competent; their assessment of a situation is accurate and rapid. Strategic leaders are adaptable; they can change their plans and their thinking as the situation changes. Strategic leaders are decisive; once they make a decision they follow up promptly. Up to the point of decision, however, leaders are collaborative; they invite, encourage, and genuinely consider suggestions from everyone. Yet strategic leaders are also commanding; their style does not invite dissent. Strategic leaders accept responsibility for the results—win, lose, or draw.

This isn't to imply that leaders never make mistakes. They do—and sometimes those mistakes are dire. Perseverance and recoverability are more important to leaders than infallibility, particularly since no one is infallible and the myth of infallibility can give rise to unrealistic expectations. Leaders also make the most of unexpected opportunities. Their can-do attitude and self-confidence allow them to take advantage of circumstances and lucky breaks. Fortune is indeed the product of a prepared mind.

Strategic Leaders and Teams

Strategic leaders inspire others in a group to do their best, raising the performance level of the whole team. In addition to heading a group effort, good leaders effectively and efficiently mold the unit into a productive and proactive team. They balance the shared goals and procedures of the group while continuing to recognize and appreciate everyone's independence. They know that mutual support is key to realizing both their own goals as well as the team's. They make it clear that everybody will share in the work and in the reward, so they don't waste precious time struggling over who controls what turf.

> ARE YOU A GOOD TEAM PLAYER, OR DO YOU FIND IT CHALLENGING? IF YOU ARE A TEAM LEADER, ARE YOU EFFECTIVE?

Traditionally, North American corporations have been very hierarchical, with a handful of top executives making all the decisions. This vertical and rigidly narrow structure is giving way to collaborative and cross-functioning departments, however, because that's what it takes to stay on top in the global race to succeed. In today's rapidly changing and highly competitive world, organizations are under the gun to deliver results faster and with fewer mistakes than ever before. Instant worldwide communication means that in some cases, tightly knit teams may do all their work by teleconferencing and e-mail, and never even see each other.

> IF YOU'VE WORKED ON CROSS-FUNCTIONAL TEAMS, DID YOU FIND THIS TO BE A REWARDING EXPERIENCE? HOW HAVE YOU HELPED OR HINDERED THE TEAM'S PRODUCTIVITY?

Such far-flung operations make teamwork and leadership even more important. Companies are realizing that empowering everyone and making them feel like part of the team is not only thoughtful and humanitarian, it's really good for business: happy people are harder working and more stable than unhappy ones. As this continues, it will make it easier for you to find a corporate context compatible with your inner self.

Companies today are on the lookout for employees who not only fit in with the corporate culture and have the necessary skills, but who also demand excellence and work harmoniously in a team environment. What sacrifices have you made, and what obstacles have you overcome in order to be an effective team player? Perhaps you've thrived on your own personal achievements and recognition in the past. In order to be an effective team member, you have to control your hunger for personal recognition.

More than likely, if you aren't participating in a cross-functional or multidisciplinary team today, you will surely be a member on one in the near future. These teams are very successful in that they offer flexibility, speed, control, and multidisciplinary knowledge. Members of these teams bring different abilities, expertise, and experiences from their various organizational departments.

IS IT EASY FOR YOU TO EMBRACE DIFFERING PERSPECTIVES AND EXPERIENCES OF OTHERS?

If you hesitate to embrace teamwork, collaboration, shared values, and a willingness to be open to new ideas, the future of your career could be in jeopardy. Your ability to agree on goals, purposes, to offer input, solve problems, and make decisions are all important to your survival in your organization. Your team members may have differing perspectives; therefore, conflict is likely to arise. Effective team leaders act more as people who contribute to the team, rather than someone who manages the team—a coach and a liaison to senior management. A leader articulates a clear vision of his or her team's goals, and promotes activities essential to obtaining those goals. As a leader your commitment, trust, shared understanding through open and honest communication, contribution and creativity, participative decision making, and ownership of the process and project will help not only the team and the organization forward, but you will move forward in your career and the realization of your own personal development. You win, and the company does too.

Exemplary Strategic Leadership Practices

What exactly is a strategic leader?

Strategic leadership is about people and about helping them get to a certain place—helping the organization and the individual move forward.

> HOW DO YOU FUNCTION IN THE WORKPLACE WHEN YOU'RE
> STRESSED? DO YOU REMAIN A STRATEGIC LEADER, OR DO
> YOU BECOME A MANAGER? ARE YOU AN EXEMPLARY
> STRATEGIC LEADER? DO YOU CONSISTENTLY ARTICULATE
> YOUR VALUES, FOLLOW YOUR PASSION, AND CREATE A
> SHARED VISION?

Strategic management is about the task and getting the task accomplished. When people are stressed, they tend to forget about leadership (the people) and focus on management (the task). Therein lies the problem and the challenge of leadership. To develop your exemplary strategic leadership skills, it's important to operate at all times from the "normal" mode rather than the "stress" mode.

How do you become a strategic leader?

Your strategic leadership skills are defined by the true you (i.e., your ethics, principles, and values)—your driving force in situations of all sorts. The first critical step to becoming a strategic leader is to identify and develop strategic leadership thinking skills, characteristics, and attributes as part of your overall leadership development. By using this approach, you are better able to define, identify, and develop your strategic thinking skills, which will aid in your overall success. As a strategic leader you are always thinking several steps ahead. You're proactive rather than reactive, and are able to possess and exert an increased level of power and influence in all situations. Reactions don't always have to be inevitable, though many may think so. Strategic leaders know how to make that shift by understanding themselves, and understanding their reactions to situations that push their buttons. Strategic leaders create new ways to handle challenging and uncomfortable situations—and they master this daunting task.

Strategic leaders focus on the four capitals of an organization: human (the employees), community (both local and global), resource (the money and the budget), and political. The goal of strategic leaders is to always focus on methods that allow systems to work effectively—the best fit, best mix of people. A second goal is to ensure that all people inside and outside of the organization act in concert with the organization's mission and vision, allowing a successful outcome to challenges faced by the organization, its internal customers (employees), and the external customers (vendors, collaborators, partners, and so on).

Many studies of exemplary leadership over the years confirm that the best leadership practices aren't the exclusive property of a select few.

Anyone in the workplace can be a strategic leader—a pioneering trailblazer who guides others to greater heights by taking new directions rather than following the same old paths. Great strategic leaders are like great coaches who rally their teams and inspire them to win; they motivate and mobilize you to be your personal best, leading you and your company to new heights of excellence.

My 2003 research (further corroborated by my 2007 study) uncovered the five most effective best practices of strategic leaders as offered by senior level executives, directors, and middle managers. These strategic leadership practices have common threads and are marked by patterns of action. Although all participants had experiences that were unique to their own situation, common practices of strategic leaders emerged that made them successful and effective no matter the organization or situation. The best practices of exemplary strategic leaders: 1) lead by example, 2) create, encourage, and inspire a shared vision, 3) take risks appropriately, 4) collaborate, motivate, and build trust, and 5) enable and empower others. We'll examine each of these in a little more detail.

Lead by Example

Exemplary strategic leaders lead by example, through strategic thinking, competence, attention to detail, authenticity, and congruence. As the saying goes, if you don't stand for something, you'll fall for anything. You can't lead without credibility.

> HAVE YOU FOUND YOUR OWN VOICE OF EXEMPLARY STRATEGIC LEADERSHIP THROUGH YOUR SPOKEN VALUES AND BELIEFS? ARE YOUR ACTIONS IN LINE WITH THE ORGANIZATION'S SHARED VALUES?

Leaders who have charisma and can make a great speech are on the right track, but what the world wants to see most of all are words followed by equivalent deeds, passion for the words spoken, clear commitment to beliefs, and relentless tenacity in achieving excellence for the employees and the organization. Exemplary strategic leaders have clear guiding principles and follow them daily. They are credible, authentic, and congruent: Leaders "walk the walk and talk the talk" without stuttering, faltering, or wavering. They never ask anyone to do anything they wouldn't, couldn't, or shouldn't do for themselves. The right and the respect given to a leader is a direct result of his or her ability to lead by example through action and direct involvement with individual employees.

As a strategic leader, you must give a distinct and clear voice to your values. But even before you do that, you must find your voice by leading from your values and beliefs. Leaders are never timid about letting others know what's important to them. In fact, they're quite proud of giving a voice to what it is they value. If leaders don't have values and beliefs to stand up for, then how will they create an environment where others can stand up for theirs? As an exemplary leader, you truly believe in your cause. The leadership process is a reciprocal one; it becomes successful when leaders meet their followers' expectations. Every survey participant considered this the most important of all leadership characteristics.

Create, Encourage, and Inspire a Shared Vision

Exemplary leaders create, encourage, and inspire a shared vision. They don't have to command commitment from others, they inspire it. Exemplary leaders are always scanning the horizon for opportunities. As a leader, you are a creator and change agent who accomplishes what others have been unable to do. You see clear visions for the future and enable everyone else to see them too. You're able to fill them with your passion and excitement—and if you can't do that, others will not follow you. Leaders create, encourage, and inspire a shared vision bringing everyone forward into the future, creating a change or shift in the individual and the organization. Leaders have enthusiasm that is contagious, like a gust of wind that spreads a flickering flame.

Employees must feel assured that you speak their language, have a clear concern for their interests, understand their needs, and take the necessary steps to meet them. Your constituents want to know that you understand what motivates them. Ultimately, employees, colleagues, subordinates, and coworkers want to know that their leaders see them, their visions, aspirations, hopes, and dreams, and are willing in turn to help them reach their goals by creating a unity of purpose for the whole.

Be an Appropriate Risk Taker

Exemplary strategic leaders do not keep up with the status quo. They challenge it, question it, and change the process when necessary. The best leaders are purposive strivers, pioneers who venture out, examine, and willfully tackle the unknown while challenging the system. They're innovators who love to hear about new ideas, recognizing and embracing change, taking appropriate risks, unafraid of failure. They learn how to celebrate the little successes, the incremental steps that help to build confidence in the face of big challenges.

Do you take appropriate risks and learn from your mistakes, as well as your successes?

Exemplary strategic leaders don't sit twiddling their thumbs waiting for a stroke of luck to come along. They're on the offensive, searching for ways to learn and grow. They transform and improve, and never try to hide behind an excuse. Think about a time when you've heard people at the office complaining about circumstances beyond their control. Exemplary leaders have a goal to acknowledge, accept, and learn from both their successes and failures. Good leaders stare in the face of adversity and are shaped by it for the better.

Collaborator, Motivator, and Trust Builder

Exemplary strategic leaders are great collaborators, motivators, and trust builders who foster environments allowing and enabling others to think in new and innovative ways. Great leaders are great encouragers. How often have you seen someone at work totally discouraged, unmotivated, or disenchanted because he's tired of "running on the hamster's wheel"—getting exhausted, going nowhere fast, and feeling unappreciated?

As a leader you're a collaborative motivator.

How do you encourage the hearts, dreams, and visions of others, and celebrate their successes?

You know the importance of giving people genuine encouragement. It doesn't have to be a big, dramatic gesture; a kind word or a simple compliment in front of others can mean the world to someone who feels he doesn't really matter. Encouragement makes employees' hearts and dreams come alive. As a leader, you can help others see their personal goals and your corporate goals as one and the same, or at least as compatible. You create a climate of camaraderie and encouragement that fosters that sustained behavior and performance, and subordinates align their own values with organizational ones.

Leaders connect with their superiors, subordinates, and colleagues as human beings. During challenging moments and uncertain times, they remain highly visible, getting their employees to think clearly about priorities and shared values, painting a clear picture to make values seem more tangible and realistic, working side by side and spending precious time with employees. Great leaders know that authentic celebrations, acknowledgements, and rituals build and strengthen community, motivate everyone, and get them over the hump in difficult and challenging times.

Enable and Empower Others

Exemplary leaders enable and empower others. You've all heard of the sayings: "There's no 'I' in team"; "No man is an island"; "You're only as strong as the weakest link." Yes, they're trite little phrases, but they make their point accurately and well. Great leaders know they need a great team. When you talk with someone at your office who has just completed a team project, is the focus on "I" or "we"? Do others take credit for the success? Great leaders acknowledge everyone's hard work rather than hogging the glory for themselves or lavishing praise on a favored team member.

As a leader you enable and empower others to act, inspiring them to succeed by encouraging them, standing by them, and giving them the tools they need. You think they can do it, so they think so too. Today's global economy has given us many virtual organizations, where team members seldom or never actually see each other face to face. But the same leadership standards apply.

ARE YOU A POWER SHARER, COLLABORATOR, AND MOTIVATOR? ARE YOU A BUILDER OF TRUST?

Great leaders know that being engaged with others, building trust, and fostering a collaborative climate of true teamwork and community, whether the team is actually together or not, is imperative for creating sustained success, productivity, loyalty, and commitment.

Gone are the days when companies strongly tended toward command-and-control leadership and their workers were resigned to feeling alienated, powerless, and overly dependent on others. How many times have you gone into a store to exchange or return an item and the person at the register had to call for a manager to get an approval? Does that employee feel trusted with authority, information, and discretion? Does that employee feel empowered? Is that person likely to go that extra mile for the organization or for you?

An exemplary strategic leader knows when to share power, and even when to relinquish it, which ultimately enables and empowers others. As a result, all parties involved feel a sense of ownership in the entire process, rather than as an isolated and unappreciated fragment. They feel more committed, stronger, and capable; they can't wait to give it everything they've got for you! When leaders make their constituents feel confident through building a bond and trust, the result is refreshing change, appropriate risk taking, and the entire organization moving forward as a whole. Employees become leaders in time, and everyone succeeds.

Five Steps and Beyond

We hope that success in your business career seems closer and more attainable now than ever before. We've shared our five steps to surviving and thriving in the workplace and the research our conclusions and recommendations are based on. We've introduced you to a variety of men and women facing a whole catalogue of challenges, irritations, and difficulties ranging from relatively minor to catastrophic. In their stories and examples, we hope you can see parallels with your own career. By observing what worked for them and what didn't, you may be able to clarify what will work for you. These steps we're suggesting aren't always easy, but we hope the process and the purpose are simple and clear.

The five steps we propose will work in almost any business environment we know of, but they don't always work alone. Every worker, every career, and every employer are different, so it may well be you'll want or need to go deeper and do more in order to achieve the level of satisfaction and success you seek. Part II of *Your Personal Power-Up* moves beyond these five essential steps to a series of additional tips you can use as the need arises. The steps in Part I are for almost anyone in any job. The resources and information in Part II are more specific. We hope you'll read the ones that apply to you in order to reach your career goals, and that you'll read the others in order to be a better, more compassionate, more visionary member of your business team.

Action Item
• Practice and develop your exemplary strategic leadership skills.

Part II

Chapter 6: Coaching, Mentoring, and Psychotherapy

Be not afraid of growing slowly, be only afraid of standing still.

—Chinese proverb

The first stage of your journey to unlocking *Your Personal Power-Up* is complete. The five steps in Part I are for everyone, and in some cases they may be all you need:

- *Step One* is to know yourself, peeling back the layers to look at who you are, how you got to be that person, and how you developed the definition you have of yourself.

- *Step Two* is to resolve contradictions between who you are and the person others perceive you to be, identifying the labels other people assign to you and comparing them with the true you.

- *Step Three* is to embrace change while enabling yourself and others; mastering the fear of change and choosing to take an appropriate degree of risk.

- *Step Four* get comfortable, establish a workplace context (even if it's theoretical), gather workplace allies and consider your inner self in relation to your corporate environment.
- *Step Five* is Carpe Diem; Seize the day and move forward with confidence.

But how is the process different if you're a woman? What if you can't find the allies you need? What do you do if an unexpected success leads to a downward spiral? Part II offers the answers to these questions and more.

Outside Help

The first of these is how to get around seemingly impossible roadblocks by using some outside help. There are times when, no matter how faithfully you've worked through the five steps to surviving and thriving, or how faithful or effective your allies are, you need a perspective and a skill set that's set apart from the organization. As we'll see, some of the characters we've already met take this approach to get out of the ruts they've fallen into. In fact, you'll find that to move forward successfully, you need outside help more often than not.

There are three primary methods for helping yourself move forward when you're stuck in transition or trying to make a change: coaching, mentoring, and psychotherapy.

How Coaches Can Help

All coaching, whether in the conference room or on the playing field, uses focused conversation to create sustained improvement, purposeful action, and individual growth. Personalized, consistently focused coaching helps you reach your career goals by highlighting and leveraging your strengths, developing strategies for maximizing your performance, and identifying obstacles to your success. Executive coaching includes intellectual and social aspects, along with acquisition of interactional skills.

Executive coaching is an ongoing relationship enabling you to create rewarding accomplishments both in your career and personal life. It gives you a deeper understanding of yourself through education, facilitation, process development, skill enhancement, group enhancement, and other developmental processes. It can improve your performance and quality of life both at home and at work.

Executive coaching (or professional development coaching, which is similar) develops high performance leaders and fast-trackers. To make the most of every opportunity and challenge, aspiring workers need the impartial sounding board coaches can provide, offering strategies on how you can reach far beyond your assumed potential. Career development coaching helps you employ your strengths, uncover your blind spots, and identify a course of action for sustained success in your career.

Let's revisit Victoria B. (from chapter 1) and Savannah H. (from chapter 3) to see if executive coaching could help them out of their ruts. You may remember that Victoria was a domineering micromanager whose subordinates boycotted the company Christmas party, while Savannah treated people she recognized as being like herself with anger and indifference.

Victoria's direct reports rebelled even though her superiors were satisfied with her productivity. Surprised by this, her bosses directed her to have executive coaching, in the course of which Victoria recognized that she was imposing her father's experience with a tough, hard-charging female boss on her own current work situation. With the help of her coach's perspective, she quickly saw that this was inappropriate. The coach then taught her techniques that promoted a more interactive and collaborative relationship with her direct reports.

Victoria had her own ideas about enabling others to succeed—she did it on her terms and for her standards. Her justification was that she knew how to get things done and figured that all the others had to do was to follow her lead. She believed she was an enabler—until the rebellion made her realize that others had voiced some major concerns about her leadership. Victoria was misidentifying her environment as the one her father had worked in, and, most significantly, she was mislabeling her team. After the coaching process, Victoria's reports were able to replace their labels with new interactive role definitions, and life got a lot better for Victoria, her direct reports, and her superiors. Victoria learned how to enable others while not only protecting her job but excelling in it—by making sure everyone perceived her as a team player and enabler. This behavior marked her among senior executives as an invaluable—and very possibly exceptional—employee. The whole process of transformation took six months. As a result, Victoria is now a more effective manager, and the productivity of her business unit increased above its previous level.

Savannah's problems turned out to be more severe than Victoria's, and the result of her executive coaching was less successful. Savannah rose from humble beginnings, earned an Ivy League college degree, and worked her way up to the executive level of a Fortune 500 company. But she avoids other women executives like herself, botches the opportunity to head a women's leadership group, and ends up at odds with all the female employees. Savannah needs executive coaching due to the dissention within the ranks.

Unlike Victoria, Savannah chooses her own coach rather than getting one through the company. Unfortunately, this coach is an idiosyncratic advisor prone to quick fixes and unsuccessful exercises. Instead of improving the situation, Savannah's coaching makes the issues more acute, leading to increased anxiety and near panic. It turns out to be an unfortunate mismatch. A successful coach has to understand the client, have a clear grasp of the problem, and have the skills and experience to help.

Savannah's second coach is a much better fit, and emphasizes and interaction with other women. She pinpoints Savannah's distrust of women, and gives her role-playing exercises in which she practices new and more patient responses. Savannah learns that time spent with others is a key variable, and that the quality of that time depends on mutual expectations. She soon learns to recognize outliers of her own hostility, learns the technique of relaxing and talking more to women—particularly asking more questions—and inviting them to express more of their opinions and to give her more constructive feedback.

These simple techniques begin to thaw Savannah's frozen relationships, but her coach has to reinforce them, because Savannah remains inclined to resist them. Savannah will need long-term coaching; both she and her executive coach are aware that her issues go beyond the obvious and are resistant to change. Though she continues to make progress, there is clearly a gulf between what Savannah is able to accomplish and what she needs to accomplish. Maybe with time, Savannah will succeed completely, or perhaps she'll need to turn to another of our roadblock-busting sources of outside help.

Will You Let Me Be Your Shadow? The Mentoring Paradigm

Executive coaching and mentoring are somewhat similar, the chief difference being the level of interpersonal experience. At times, mentoring is more personal and more intensive than coaching, extending beyond weekly sessions and specific tasks, problems, or projects to an ongoing one-on-one relationship.

The term *mentor* comes from the man whom King Odysseus of Ithaca charged with watching over and teaching his young son. Homer's *Odyssey* tells the story: Odysseus asked his wise and trusted friend, Mentor, to act as a surrogate father to his son, Telemachus, while the king was away fighting the Trojan War. During his father's ten-year absence, Telemachus relied on Mentor to teach him both by word and example, and help him become the man he was meant to be. Other historical examples of successful mentoring dyads include Socrates and Plato, Medici and Michelangelo, Freud and Jung.

A modern business mentor/protégé relationship consists of a skilled professional taking an active interest in the career development of a lesser skilled individual. A mentor can be anyone in a position of power (relative to the protégé) who provides career-enhancing guidance and psychosocial support through encouragement, counseling, confirmation, and friendship. The objective is to help the protégé develop a sense of professional identity and greater self-confidence. The mentor also may give advice on social skills, introduce the protégé to key contacts and help the protégé navigate complex systems, particularly political systems, within a chosen profession or sphere of influence.

The protégé typically shadows his mentor on the job to watch and learn during the work experience. Mentoring goes beyond teaching physical and verbal skills, to demonstrate negotiating among and within social structures and settings to bring acquired skills to bear. Mentor and protégé relationships may continue outside the walls of a specific workplace as the mentor moves on to a different job and brings his new peer along. In the best of all worlds, the successful protégé eventually goes beyond identification with the mentor: the protégé becomes the peer.

Of course there are different degrees of mentorship and each relationship is personally and individually defined. Like all relationships, the mentor/protégé relationship develops over time. Initially, there may be a great deal of imitation and identification with the mentor, but as the protégé learns and develops both skill and confidence, his or her personal style comes into its own.

Mentors and protégés need not always share the same race, economic status, or gender, but programs should strive to reduce the social distance between the two. Mentors tend to choose protégés with whom they can identify, thereby limiting the opportunities for mentoring relationships with those who are somehow different. It isn't possible for mentors and protégés to enjoy authentic collaboration without an understanding of the forces that shape their interactions. Both sides can improve the mentoring relationship by willingness to be open to individual differences. We'll come back to this point in later chapters when we look more closely at how race and gender affect the process of choosing or becoming a mentor.

George R., a Masked Man
George R., a fifty-year-old senior engineer of Filipino-American decent with two master's degrees, has worked in a global high tech company for eight years, surviving three rounds of downsizing in the process. When he was a boy, George learned to "wear a mask" in public because he was embarrassed by his foreign-sounding name and accent: he thought he ought to be somebody other than who he really was. Though as a child he was outspoken around his peers, he was taunted by bullies, and taught by his strict parents that children should be seen and not heard. Little wonder then, that as an adult George operates "under the radar" to keep his job by not drawing attention to himself.

The culture within the team of engineers George manages is historically one that cares about employees and their families, trusts workers to accomplish their jobs, and treats everyone with dignity and respect. The organization empowers its people and gives them a sense of security, recognizes employees' accomplishments, and inspires loyalty. Even during recessionary times, the company asks its employees to take Fridays off and cut vacation time instead of downsizing. The company seems to spare no expense with training, development, and retention of its greatest assets—the employees.

But during yet another downturn in the economy, the organization begins to change. Competition replaces collaboration and flextime and profit sharing disappear. A senior executive tells George to stop babying his team and start making them produce more by creating a climate of competition. "This isn't the family-friendly company that started in a garage. The name of the game is survival!"

Uncomfortable with this new direction, George recalls his childhood memories of being bullied. Instead of rising up as a strong leader, instead of valuing himself and his team by articulating his dissatisfaction with the new corporate culture, George becomes the scared little boy again and walks around with his tail between his legs. In order to survive, he shuts up and says nothing to his manager. He cracks the whip on his team, tells them to ask no questions, and demands that they take on the competitive persona required. This not only surprises George's team, they're shocked, dismayed, and appalled that such a seemingly decent man would do such an about-face and not take their thoughts and feelings into consideration.

One evening George sits at home with his head in his hands wondering, *Why can't I be more aggressive in expressing my concerns for me and my team?* He knows he needs some answers. He feels that his career and life are stagnant. He turns to an executive coach, who tells him that fear has stifled his ability to articulate his concerns to others. The coach suggests that he also seek a mentor in his organization for added support and guidance.

George finds a male mentor at work who is a purposive striver and authentic as well. He is realistic and encouraging and doesn't betray confidences. Working with his mentor, George builds stronger self-esteem and confidence in new and anxiety-provoking situations, such as how to speak up the correct way when he disagrees. He also develops stronger communication skills, enabling him to have a clearer sense of what questions to ask when and where. His mentor monitors his progress and encourages goals and accountability, enabling George to become a more productive manager. Eventually George sees himself as the authentic person he has always been. Finally, he takes off the mask. Productivity and morale increase, and the team marches forward despite the bad times.

Mentors: The Career Makers

In the past, mentoring was an informal process, and it still is in many cases. One of my research participants said, "I wish that we had a formal mentoring program in my company. If I want a mentor, I have to find someone who is willing to be a mentor to me. I've been with my organization for twenty years and I'm still in sales. My talents haven't been fully developed." There was a time when senior executives chose protégés based on whether they were likeable or reminded them of the days gone by. Often, protégés found their mentors through the "good ol' boy" network, and grooming and developing these relationships took place over cigars or golf. Mentors, predominately Caucasian and male, gravitated toward protégés like themselves, to the detriment of women and people of color (whether male or female), who were underrepresented in corporate America.

My research found that Caucasians received promotions quickly through early fast-tracking, while people of color didn't move up in a similar way until they reached the middle management level. I found that managers of color who received promotions had close long-term support from powerful corporate sponsors and a network of strong dedicated mentors.

The globalization of business in the twenty-first century has shown today's corporations the importance of attracting, retaining, and developing talent of every age, race, and gender. Though there's still plenty of room for improvement, many organizations now fully support formal mentoring programs to ensure everyone an equal opportunity for success. Although framed by the corporate dynamic, formal mentoring programs depend on the personal relationship between participants to be successful.

DO YOU HAVE SOMEONE IN YOUR ORGANIZATION WHO PROVIDES AND FOSTERS A SAFE, NONJUDGMENTAL PLACE TO ASK QUESTIONS AND LEARN? DO YOU PAY IT FORWARD?

Mentors are a safe harbor in that they will answer the questions that you may not necessarily wish to ask your superior or boss. You may need a shield or "air cover" before you go into battle. Mentors can see those turbulent waters before you can, and steer you clear or give you shelter from the storm. Your mentor can show you the best way to approach your boss or another executive by providing tactical information. You may not have access to specific information you need to move you forward in your career. A mentor will show you all the ropes: both the tangible and intangible; both the implicit and explicit rules. If you're a new employee, you may find it difficult to interpret the mechanics of your organization. Mentors provide insight to the mechanics, structure, and nuances of your new corporate context. Working long hours may not be enough to get you where you'd like to go in your career. Your mentor may be able not only to help you position yourself in the right place and time when an opportunity comes available, but also make sure you're prepared to advance into leadership status and upward mobility when the chance arises.

Are We All Going Crazy? The Psychotherapy Paradigm

Psychotherapy is the most complex of the three options for helping you overcome workplace obstacles. If an executive coach or mentor can't give you the help you need, psychotherapy is a viable next step. Psychotherapy is a broad term describing different kinds of help that might come from a social worker, psychologist, or psychiatrist, usually in private and confidential sessions. This process requires a competent mental health professional who is usually licensed or certified by the state. The local chapter of the American Psychiatric Association, American Psychological Association, and local medical doctors are effective referral sources that can help you.

Psychotherapy addresses more deeply rooted personality and self-identity issues. At first someone undergoing this process may identify with and emulate the therapist, but it's expected that the person will eventually acquire his or her own insight into motives and expectations. This process is called insight therapy. When the client seems too fragile for insight therapy, or doesn't want it, supportive and educational therapies, such as those modeled after Alcoholics Anonymous, offer other options.

A good indicator that you might benefit greatly from this kind of professional help would be that you have symptoms of depression or anxiety that persist despite the use of other methods. Mental health is like physical health in that it's a great idea to get a check-up periodically. And if you feel sick, get help! There is (and should be) decreasing stigma attached to professional psychological counseling. That's probably because there are very few of us who haven't needed or sought a little extra help from time to time. As we move forward, we'll help you see which type of support, if any, might be appropriate for you. Let's revisit one of our characters from earlier in the book who got a fresh start from psychotherapy after it seemed that all was lost.

Jimmy C., Redux

Jimmy C. was the promising senior marketing manager in chapter 1 who buckled under the pressure to succeed and fell into the cultural stereotype of the drunken Irishman. Let's take a look at him now. At first things appeared pretty hopeless: he lost his job and ended up living out of his car for a few months. What happened to the resilient young man with so much on the ball? The good news is that the sharp, hard-working Jimmy is still there beneath his current labels of troublemaker, drunkard, beggar, and homeless person.

As luck would have it, Jimmy is befriended by a priest who works with the homeless and sees still untapped potential and the remnants of a striving self beneath Jimmy's current labels. Through an outreach program for the homeless, and with the priest as his mentor, Jimmy moves into a halfway house that understands the ravages of substance abuse, addiction, and alcoholism.

As part of this program, Jimmy begins psychotherapy with a nontraditional therapist who is also an amateur boxer. His therapist is fascinated by the unconscious alignment of Jimmy's self with great Irish warriors—which has led him to an interest and significant knowledge of the history of boxing in general. During the course of treatment, the therapist draws attention to the fact that in boxing (indeed, in all sport), losses occur—but that true sportsmen keep fighting on, rather than giving up.

With these cautious first insights, Jimmy slowly begins to reassert his own identity. The process takes about a year and, in reality, is a continuing effort. The therapist suggests Jimmy end therapy at about the same time Jimmy is leaving the halfway house. He bolsters Jimmy's self-confidence by saying that he can do it on his own—but if not, he can come back.

A female volunteer in the halfway house notices Jimmy's good humor. She's an executive with an international sports manufacturer and once she learns of his prior work experience, offers him a starting position as a buyer. It is during this time that Jimmy's striving self begins to reemerge. Feeling bad and guilty about losing the old career that he cherished, Jimmy begins to make a concerted effort to prove to himself and his former manager and teammates that he can once again be a reliable successful member of the team. In the end, with lots of hard work and his learned introspective skills, Jimmy regroups, interviews for his old position, and gets his job back!

His family—so relieved by his "return"—proves much more flexible than you might expect. Jimmy, having moved from his labeled position in the family, discovers that he had a secret ally all along—his mother. And she, now sensing the freedom to express things she could not before, turns out to be in her own way a rebel.

Jimmy's dropping of old labels and adoption of a new role produces not only changes in his workplace but also significant differences in how his family relates to him. Jimmy is clearly on his way!

What outside help would you have selected for each of these characters—Victoria, Savannah, George, and Jimmy? It's actually possible to justify any of them for any of the people. Psychotherapy may seem to be the most potent. It is not necessarily always the right answer because we are complex. It seems clear that all of our characters need to interact with another human being in order to act against the negative self. How do you feel about each of these forms of personal assistance? Which of them would best help you remove your roadblock? (Perhaps all you'll need to do is read this book!)

Action Item
- Find out what source of assistance is available in your organization if needed.

Chapter 7: Avoiding the Downside of Success

Pray that success will not come any faster than you are able to endure it.

—Benjamin Nnamdi Azikiwe, president of Nigeria (1904–1996)

How can there be any downside to success? The idea seems almost unimaginable. Success is the goal we've been talking about and the objective most of us are chasing throughout our working lives. Yet, as you may have experienced yourself, success of all sorts drags unexpected problems along with it. When the good things come, the bad things may not be far behind.

For example, at first glance it would seem that winning the lottery is a good thing. Suddenly you've got more money that you ever imagined possible, and it's yours to do whatever you want with. Along with all those millions, however, come family, friends, and complete strangers by the dozens popping out of the woodwork and asking for money. Right behind the huge financial windfall comes a huge tax bill. And just because the lucky winners have money doesn't mean they know how to invest it wisely. Some big winners end up more broke than they were to begin with, or even in trouble with the law because they got too deeply in debt. In extreme cases, people say their life was much simpler before the big payday and wish it had never happened.

Many times success contains the seeds of failure. It introduces the temptation, if not the necessity, to change your self to fit the new expectations others have of you because of your success. This calls for a varied authentication of your core self, or what we can term a *newly authenticated self*. You will have many authentications of your core self in the course of your life and career, and the trick is to hang on to your core identity through all of them. Unfortunately, as you stack one success on top of another, your negative self comes along for the ride. You may remember from chapter 3 that the negative self is the ultimate anchor of status quo behavior, a sense of anxiety and immobility that clings to the familiar but fears the new. When success plops you down in a new work context or saddles you with heightened expectations from others, the negative self can bring your winning streak to an abrupt and painful halt. The way to keep this from happening is to know your negative self and know how to deal with it successfully.

Beth's Conflict With Success

Beth is a success, but she doesn't feel like one. An overachiever and a perfectionist of sorts, she is vice president of research and development for a multinational corporation. At forty-four, Beth has lost her job three times over the years due to downsizings and reorganizations, but her current employer recruited her from an executive director post at another company. Each time Beth was downsized she became a little less confident, feeling her self-esteem being chipped away bit by bit. She blames herself for her failure, though she knows in each case it was a matter of economics, not her job performance.

Beth's father taught her that she should never allow others to limit her, and never limit herself. *Excellence is everything* was his philosophy. "People don't have to like you, but they do have to respect you," he told her. This was in sharp contrast to her mother's belief that a woman should be content to be "a great man's lady" and not try to go beyond the status quo. The two differing parental voices conflict within Beth. While she appears confident on the outside, she's always apprehensive and unsure of herself on the inside, in spite of her workplace success.

As Beth prepares to deliver an important presentation to her colleagues and superiors, she recalls a quotation her father told her to remember when she's afraid. The famous line from "Invictus" by William Ernest Henley reads, ". . . I am the master of my fate: I am the captain of my soul."[1]

Reciting these words to herself as she steps to the lectern, Beth makes a successful presentation. But, once again, it doesn't feel like a success to her. It seems like she doesn't really belong anywhere. A fear of being judged always looms over her like a dark cloud just before a storm; her happiness at accomplishing something is invariably short-lived. Instead of satisfaction in a job well done, success has brought Beth stress and discomfort.

Beth's colleagues, superiors, subordinates, and friends describe her as confident, successful, highly intelligent, collaborative, tenacious, and a risk taker, always immaculately dressed, and professional. However, Beth thinks of herself as shy, introverted, and proactive almost to a fault. She demands loyalty from those around her, but is insecure about who she really is or where her future is headed.

Unfortunately Beth isn't quite as proactive as she thinks. While she always looks out for others, she fails to protect herself and doesn't see to it that others perceive her as one who enables success in her coworkers. She makes sure that people around her have mentors, get a chance to develop into leaders, and ultimately earn promotions. However, she doesn't do the same for herself. When the time comes for other people to help protect her, they are always trying to save their own hides. Remembering what her father said about demanding respect from others, Beth wants to be liked as well as respected. She's always looking for that external validation from others. Because she is so conflicted, she gives in rather quickly to others; later regretting her decision, she becomes angry. How will Beth overcome the downside of success? You'll learn more later.

Where the Rubber Meets the Road: What is Success?

True success comes from satisfying the requirements of your job while projecting your core identity out into the environment. If the only measures of success were external—money, job title, and so forth—the process of succeeding would always redefine the successful person. The acid test of success is whether or not you achieve success on the inside. There's a whole industry out there telling the unwary masses how to redefine themselves in order to fit into a niche, even if it means lying to others and to yourself about who you really are and what's important to you. By now we hope you know that sort of approach is a recipe for disaster. Succeeding on the outside with a made-up self on the inside is not success at all. William, our next subject, is a case and point.

Winsome Will: A Lost Identity Rediscovered

William is an aircraft engineer who spends 70 percent of his time on the road. He is highly competent, and knows that his good looks and charisma are responsible in part for his success. When his company begins contracting with the military, William's reliance on his charisma to achieve success eventually turns him into a philanderer. William exudes inspired confidence. In fact, he becomes so successful that he no longer questions himself technically or administratively. He becomes the final arbiter on his business transactions because both sides always accept his recommendations. This success leads to a career-threatening crisis.

Sent to a conference of the touchy-feely team-building variety, William tries to project his usual charisma, but a female team leader returns his confident smile with a hard stare. Usually women fall all over him, but this time his approach backfires. William is unable to charm anyone or otherwise dominate the conference. Panicked by the response, William calls a female colleague for advice. She helps him resolve the temporary crisis and refers him to a therapist for a brief intervention. William returns to work, though the more deeply rooted problem beneath the evident problem on the surface takes longer to resolve.

What happened? William, a basically good man, was perverted by his success and came to rely almost solely on his external attributes to achieve success on the job and get through life. The availability of women who hero-worshiped him and men who seldom questioned him turned a good but needy person into an exploiting hypocrite. The conference gave William the eye-opening opportunity to encounter himself without anyone giving prior deference to his walk-in identity. You might say that William's better self was looking for a chance to reassert its dominance. Success spoiled him, but self-knowledge and a will to succeed, in terms of a long-negated core self, reestablished a decent and well-functioning individual. By most any measure, the new improved William is a better person than the one who had been accustomed to getting by with his flawed definition of success, based upon charisma laden with a heavy dose of philandering intent.

The Celebrity Trap

Celebrities are a special case when it comes to lost identity and the pitfalls of success. There's little question that the perks of fame include favorable presumptions from juries, judges, and law enforcement professionals because these authorities fail to distinguish between the celebrity image and the real person behind it who breaks the law. Because of this star power, the celebrities themselves begin to lose the distinction between self and projection. Sometimes the results can have historic implications. During the notorious McCarthy hearings in the 1950s, when a congressional panel grilled film industry figures looking for Communist sympathizers, movie stars including Humphrey Bogart and Robert Taylor assumed their tough-guy personas, which only reaffirmed the committee's belief that there were Communist infiltrators in Hollywood.

Their Definitions or Yours: Should You Leave Your Roots Behind?

The popular and highly successful 1957 film *Will Success Spoil Rock Hunter* depicts a nerdish title character, played by Tony Randall, who succeeds against all odds in mounting the corporate ladder in television, which was the hot consumer technology of the 1950s.

Rock Hunter is enticed by all of the perks a fictional big shot of the 1950s could want, including the obligatory busty blonde (Jayne Mansfield) as part of the reward structure. Yet in true Capra-esque style (though it's not a Frank Capra film), the nerd remains true to himself and to his hometown girl in the end. He schemes his way to the top and becomes company president, but once he's achieved that success, he realizes he really doesn't want it. He desperately needed help from Jayne Mansfield's character in advancing his career, but he had no interest in marrying her. His "success" in the corporate world almost ruined his life.

Hunter's success brought risk and the threat of a reemergence of his negative self. A more modern movie example that demonstrates how a person's view of and reaction to success can produce disastrous results is the award-winning *American Beauty*.

> WHAT IS YOUR DEFINITION OF SUCCESS? HOW IS YOUR DEFINITION OF SUCCESS PLAYED OUT IN YOUR CAREER AND PERSONAL LIFE? IS THERE A CONFLICT BETWEEN THE TWO?

The married couple in the story has all of the appearances of success: a child, a home, cars, status, and money. The husband, played by Kevin Spacey, is a successful executive who's absolutely miserable, partly because he can't define success for himself. Eventually he goes against the grain, quits his job, and enjoys working at a fast-food restaurant. The wife, played by Annette Bening, daily repeats her company's mantra of what success looks like, and it begins to define her. She embraces the fact that success is defined for her by external forces and not her true inner self. Her husband continuously points out the fact that she isn't the carefree person that she used to be. Everyone is unhappy and eventually the family unit is destroyed. This is an extreme example that's all too common in real life.

Success can lead you to compromise the integral aspects of your self-identity, embodying attributes such as integrity, honesty, and trustworthiness—those very aspects of your core self that it is most important to maintain in all of the authentications. Like failure, success seems prone to make the human moral/ethical position worse instead of better. Failure often results from the successful reassertion of the negative self, that amalgam of maladaptive personal attributes, out-of-place and out-of-time labels and definitions, and previously identified derogatory feelings about yourself. Success brings new pressures and expectations that let the negative self reemerge and set the stage for failure down the road.

Let's meet Max J. to demonstrate how success can sometimes conspire against you.

Max J.: The Penny-Pincher

Max J. is a fifty-year-old Caucasian male University of Iowa graduate with a master's degree in finance and international relations. In the five years he has worked for a consumer products giant, he has been promoted twice. Max's parents both came from working-class families and are proud of their middle-class status. They taught Max never to take anything for granted and to save as much money as possible because "any day it can be taken away." Consequently, in his personal life Max pinches every penny as though it were his last, in an unending effort to be financially independent.

Most recently, Max's employer promoted him to regional vice president, where he oversees four regional directors of operations; each has an average of seven years at the company. The new responsibility represents a big success for Max, but that success has led to trouble. The regional directors are unhappy because they don't get enough money to run their departments properly. Turnover is high, but those who leave the company are branded as misfits. When his team approaches him about low morale, low productivity, and other hazards of the fear-based culture that has developed, Max turns a deaf ear. Max's mother always told him to roll with the punches and never complain, and he expects his subordinates to do the same.

During a regional meeting, Max vehemently defends his decisions about the budget, and comes off looking like part of the problem instead of part of the solution. Wanting to be fair, Max speaks with his superior, Arnold, about his directors' complaints. Although Arnold recognizes Max as a highly valued top performer, he sees that his team lacks the trust and respect they need to function effectively, efficiently, and productively. Arnold tells Max that he himself is always conscious about his own issues regarding money, how he distributes it within his own family, and how his feelings about money affect the way he distributes it in the workplace.

"Conduct a team-building exercise," Arnold suggests. "Sit down and talk with your team so you can fully understand who they are, what they need, and the rationale for their decisions." Both Max and Arnold meet with his regional directors and ask a series of questions based on the idea that there is a relationship between the way the participants personally handle money and the decisions they make in the workplace as a result of past teachings.

They ask the team four questions:

1. How do you define success?
2. If you had an abundance of money, how would you distribute it?
3. What did your parents/guardians teach you about money, and how is this reflected in your views regarding money today?

4. What is the role of money in your definition of success? How important is attaining happiness and a sense of self-worth in relation to your definition of success?

Here are the answers Max's regional directors gave.

- Olivia W., Asian-American female, age 35

> *Success is being happy, healthy, and secure in myself. It's not all about money. If I had a lot of money I save some, donate one-third to charities, give money to my family, and buy expensive things for myself such as homes, cars, and clothing.*
>
> *My parents taught me to spend my money wisely, and to hold on to it because it isn't easy to come by and once it's gone, it's gone. Today I take their advice. I was planning a big shopping weekend in San Francisco with my girlfriends, but on the trip I only bought items I really needed—even though I am very comfortable—because in the back of my mind I was constantly thinking about what my parents taught me.*
>
> *Money does not buy happiness. I place a high value on happiness with family, friends, connecting with people throughout my life, the joy I get from planting flowers and seeing them grow, and the satisfaction I receive from accomplishing things. I've always had enough, so money is not a central concern. My parents had lots of money. I've gotten almost whatever I've wanted throughout my life. My self-worth is not defined by the amount of money that I have received or will ever receive. My self-worth is more meaningful than any amount of money.*

You can infer that the teachings of Olivia's parents have an important effect on her feelings about money in her personal life and in the workplace. She has an abundance of it, but she also spends it hesitantly. Olivia has mixed feelings about money. On the one hand it is a simple matter because she's always had more than enough. On the other hand, the management of what she has can be complex, and an important way to remain secure within her life.

- Joe L., Black male, age 52

    Success is what you make it. It's all relative.

    I do have a lot of money, and I first give money to my family, charities, my church, and myself. Money is not that important to me, and if it were gone tomorrow, I would pick myself up and start making money again. My wealth is the product of my capacity to think. Every honest man tries to make money to the extent of his ability. When I say "honest man" I mean the one who knows that he can't consume more than he has produced. Money, to me, is simply a way to survive and obtain some of the finer things in life; nothing more, nothing less.

    My parents taught me that money is very important because it separates the haves from the have-nots. I learned that saving is of the utmost importance because being a Black man in this society, you are very lucky and blessed to simply survive; therefore, the more money you save, the more of life you will be able to enjoy. I do save a lot of my money, but I also spend a lot of it in order to enjoy life, because you can't take it with you.

    Regarding the relative importance of money in my life, I've always been taught that those who have a lot of it will find it difficult to get into heaven. Therefore, I do everything that I can in order to help my fellow man. Money does enable me to see others who are less fortunate smile, and that makes me very happy. But money won't buy intelligence for the fool, admiration for the coward, or respect for the incompetent. Money is merely a means of survival.

    I am a man who has been fortunate to make something of myself and obtain lots of money in the process. It is very important for me to tell everyone that I meet to never give up on your dreams and your goals. I am now living my dream and I can say that now that I have all of the money that I could want, it has not changed me. I'm rich with or without money.

Probably because of what Joe's parents taught him, money is only important to him to an extent. It is important in order to survive and to gain respect. Joe's legacy is one of stability, security, and religion. He has learned that giving is much better than receiving, and he tries to live his life in that manner. In the workplace, Joe makes the decision to allot monies wherever needed.

- Carolyn V., Caucasian female, age 28

> *Success is very personal. I don't allow money or material things to define me. I view myself as successful when I'm happy with myself, my life, and my surroundings.*
>
> *If I had millions of dollars, I would give the bulk of it to my family, and the rest to charity. The top priority for me is to be the best human that I can be. I would like to become a millionaire some day in order to help others. I also want to leave a legacy behind for my children.*
>
> *My parents taught me that the number one priority in my life is to place family first, treat everyone with respect, and save, save, save! They also taught me that money is never more important than your family, and if any family member is ever in need, I must help them because money can be here today and gone tomorrow. Family is forever. My parents taught me the importance of money as it relates to survival. I do not have any idea of my parents' income, because my parents felt that it was not important enough to discuss it. Today, I view money the same way that my parents view it, as a means of survival, comfort, and helping others.*
>
> *Money is important to me because it provides a source of security, stability, and allows me to help others in need. Money certainly does not buy happiness, but it allows you to have choices that you might not have. I am a very spiritual person and I know that money is both good and evil. If you do not protect yourself and know your values, priorities, and goals in life, money can be very harmful.*

You can see that Carolyn's parents did not discuss money openly and religion plays a very large role relating to her attitude towards money. Her legacy shows that her past is important and she wants to hold on to the values taught by her parents. Because she had two secure parents at home, holding on to money and not enjoying it is not something that plagues her. She is willing to spend and be happy, but she knows the importance of saving money also.

- Team Leader: Max J., Caucasian male, age 50

> *Success to me means being able to enjoy the fruits of your labor, having everything in abundance, and never worrying about where your next meal is going to come from, or how your next bill is going to be paid. If I had lots of money, I would save lots of it first. Money is a means of survival and allows us to make others happy. Therefore, I would give it to those that I cared about and those who were in need.*
>
> *I was taught to save every penny for a rainy day; I buy and spend only when necessary for food, shelter, and clothing. My parents taught me that it's better to have a savings account because money is hard to get, and that's a way of hanging on to it. Their teachings have influenced the way I view money today. I hold on to money and spend it wisely. I have taught my children the same thing. It is important to save for the unexpected.*
>
> *Money greatly impacts security, although it does not ensure it. Most of my attention is focused on enrichment and growth and happiness, not money. If I didn't have any money, I'd still be happy, because that is who I am. Money will not add or subtract from my self-worth. It does not mean very much my self-worth. I am who I am, and nothing will change that. If I had lots of money tomorrow, I'd be the same person. Money is not the root of evil, but it certainly changes people. If I had lots of money, it would allow me to live comfortably, and that's all it means to me.*

You may notice that Max is contradicting himself here. He is very conservative in his spending due to his parents' teachings. He says that he spends money on the necessities such as food and clothing. Despite his announcement concerning independence and generosity in his personal life, he holds on tightly to money. He fully believes that money does not come around very easily and you must work hard for it. Is that attitude spilling out into the workplace and causing trouble for his direct reports?

Looking over the meeting results, Max discovers that money is important to the team as a way of survival, but it is not so important that having more of it will make them change. Team members with issues about money in their personal life may end up withholding adequate fiscal supplies to department heads and subordinates or may award money lavishly. Some may require a demonstration of the "right" to have money distributed to others. All the team members speak about their legacies, telling stories that place family above most other things. They reveal that their past teachings are very pertinent to the way they live their lives and make decisions today.

THINK ABOUT MAX AND HIS DIRECT REPORTS. REFLECT ON THEIR CONFLICTS AND THE SOURCE OF THEIR CONFLICTS CENTERING ON MONEY, SUCCESS, HERITAGE, AND CULTURAL BELIEFS. NOW TURN YOUR THOUGHTS INWARD. WHAT IS THE SOURCE OF YOUR CONFLICTS? HOW HAVE HERITAGE AND CULTURAL BELIEFS IMPACTED YOU IN YOUR PERSONAL AND PROFESSIONAL LIFE AS IT RELATES TO MONEY AND SUCCESS?

We want to feel that we're in control of our money, but money subtly exercises control over us. Clearly, executives like Max ought to spend their discretionary budget based on what's best for the company and not what reflects their personalities. To continue to succeed, Max has to resolve the conflict between his personal viewpoint and his professional responsibility.

Is Max's work with Arnold sufficient enough to move him beyond the negative aspects of self that are causing him so much trouble? In this case, all it takes is interaction with another human being and enough emotional intelligence to get beyond the hold of the negative self—the penny-pinching, money-grubbing Max whose existence he denies. Max is a highly intelligent man with a fair degree of self-knowledge and emotional intelligence. With help from his boss, Max escapes the grasp of the negative self in the workplace and continues on his path to success.

> IF YOU COULD ONLY EXPERIENCE THE JOY OF SUCCESS AND NEVER EXPERIENCE FAILURE IN YOUR CAREER AND LIFE, WHAT WOULD YOU DO AND WHAT WOULD YOU LEARN FROM IT?

Clearly when the fiscal discussion brings in unrecognized early family structural issues and teachings, resolution between team members becomes unlikely. It is a leadership responsibility to be free enough of that to be able to lead the dialogue to a different basis.

It Hurts So Badly: Sometimes Success and Failure Feel the Same

Reviewing the characters we've met in this chapter, we see that Beth, though highly successful, perceives her success through an unnecessary haze of pain. Max, while initially successful, destroys his success and can't see that he's doing so. William deviates from a standard of behavior set early in life and jeopardizes his career. In each case, the negative self is responsible for the difficulties these people face in the wake of success. It's little wonder then why success for these three feels so much like failure, and ultimately, in fact, gives way to failure. You may be tempted to think that if you're successful you're happier or have a better, more fulfilled and comfortable life with fewer problems and headaches than when you're experiencing what appears to be failure. We tend not to realize that success brings its own unique set of concerns. Success and failure have overlapping workplace and personal issues, whether they center on leadership, fiscal matters, programming hurdles, staffing, or other difficulties.

Imagine celebrating victory on a big team by focusing on yourself instead of the team. Rather than congratulating and rewarding everyone involved, as team leader you claim all the glory as your own. In reality it was the team that was a success; however, by focusing on yourself, not only do you place a great amount of stress on yourself, you send the message that the other team members weren't so important. That deflates the spirit of the team, making failure much more likely the next time around. Suddenly the seeds of failure are planted in the midst of success.

Typically a certain amount of conflict emerges when you're trying to accomplish a task. Then when you're finished, it may be that some of your team members aren't too happy with the result; it's seldom the case that everybody is completely satisfied in the end. There may be someone saying, "We shouldn't have done it this way," and a chorus of second-guessing or Monday morning quarterbacking. The team has realized its dream of success, and now some of the members are disappointed because the grass that looked so green before is suddenly turning a little brown.

Another point to consider is that success raises the stakes. When your team is successful you'll need newer, bigger, louder, and brighter bells and whistles that require more resources, structure, and efficiency maintained at higher levels. And by the way, to maintain that new level of success, you'll need more energy. Redefined staff and leadership roles use more energy, with some of that energy producing success and some, paradoxically, leading to failure.

Success brings with it a propensity for your momentum to either peak or slow down. Think about that big team project you perfected. Were you totally exhausted and elated at the same time? Did you feel that you needed rest and relaxation or a celebration? You and your team both need a rest after you've finished a big job. But you know that if you rest too long after a workout, you may not want to get back up. Once you're successful, it takes time to get the momentum going and the juices flowing again.

Stretched to Success

Have you ever had one success after another and then all of a sudden been blindsided by an unexpected failure? How did you and your team members feel? What happened to your momentum? Most likely you were disappointed, and may have spent your energy pointing the finger at somebody else. You can't always be a success, but you can overcome the failures and get back on the path toward success in the future.

There are times when being *stretched to success*—going beyond everything you thought possible to meet an objective—causes so much stress and trauma that the whole team collapses in the end; workers quit because they don't think they can recover from the experience. Organizations regularly lose good people because of this. They may decide it's too hard to transform and adapt to their organization's cutting edge changes; it's easier to go to work for the competition.

HAVE YOU EVER EXPERIENCED A PARADOXICAL FEELING OF FAILURE AFTER ATTAINING SUCCESS? CONTINUE TO REFLECT ON YOUR THOUGHTS.

Success brings some responsibilities and leadership challenges that you can anticipate and others that you can't. It can make previously exemplary leadership obsolete. Success may demand new levels of skills, energy, and ability that the previously successful leader doesn't have. If a leader isn't quite ready to take on those new responsibilities and challenges, employees who have counted on that leader to reach a particular level of success may see that he or she won't be able to get there. That means that there are times when teams or companies feel no choice but to leave a respected leader behind.

No doubt your organization has decided at one time or another to make a change that you didn't feel comfortable with, but they told you it had to be done for the overall health of the company. In chapter 3 we looked at the inevitability of change in today's global corporate marketplace. In chapter 5 we saw that there are times when you have to reexamine your commitment and loyalty to your organization. Some see the success-induced changes as a time to start fresh somewhere else; others stay, grooming themselves for growth in the next stage, while simultaneously reinforcing and strengthening the organization's momentum.

Leaving the Negative Self Behind

In dealing with the threat of failure in the midst of success, Beth, Max, William, and other examples illustrate how strongly the negative self affects your prospects for success, and how much of the negative self is shaped by childhood experiences. Therefore our goal and focus now is to review and expand on the attributes or characteristics of the negative self as discussed in chapter 3, and learn how to identify the messages that run like constant dialogues inside your head, causing disruptive feelings throughout your career and personal life.

> DO YOU HAVE AN ACCURATE VIEW OF YOURSELF? HOW IS THAT LONG-HELD VIEW IMPACTING YOU TODAY IN YOUR CAREER AND PERSONAL LIFE?

Personal trolls, personal demons: voices of the negative self

Let's take a look at how you can you identify the messages that run inside your head and cause disruptive feelings. Jitters, anxiety, and self-doubt are all normal feelings that become problems only when their presence incapacitates. On the hit '90s CBS comedy Northern Exposure, a dwarf-sized Eskimo periodically appears alongside Ed, the young would-be shaman who often grapples with feelings of unworthiness. The Green

Man, as Ed calls him, accompanies Ed everywhere, yet, no one but Ed can see him. He is the perfect embodiment of Ed's low self-esteem and self-loathing. The Green Man emotionally sabotages Ed with ceaseless diatribes, constantly telling him that he will not succeed because he is not good enough and that he is a failure, until Ed is disabled by emotional exhaustion or consumed by self-doubt and fear. No matter what Ed says or does, the Green Man won't go away. But, as the Green Man reminds Ed, "You called me." For some reason, Ed cannot let go of him. As a dramatic construct, the Green Man exemplifies perfectly the basic concept of the negative self.

> THE BELIEFS ABOUT YOURSELF THAT YOU CARRY AROUND WITH YOU ARE DERIVED FROM OTHER SOURCES. HOW DO YOU FEEL ABOUT THE SOURCES FROM WHICH YOUR BELIEFS WERE DERIVED? THINK ABOUT HOW THOSE BELIEFS ARE IMPACTING YOU TODAY.

> DO YOU HAVE AN ACCURATE VIEW OF YOURSELF? HOW IS YOUR LONG-HELD VIEW OF YOURSELF IMPACTING YOUR CAREER AND PERSONAL LIFE?

You've learned about success and failure and how they sometimes feel the same. Now let's talk about how success breeds failure. When you achieve success, you might form habits that keep you from sustained leadership. For example, if you are rewarded for a particular behavior, you might begin to believe in the status quo; you don't work harder, you just continue providing what got you the first accolades. You become complacent. Executives and leaders, in order to combat complacency, must continuously raise their performance expectations.

How does this fit in with the negative self? Low self-esteem, may cause you to have low self-confidence. If you've ever felt as though you weren't good enough to get that promotion or good evaluation, low self-esteem could be the culprit. Self-confidence is the solution.

Ninety percent of all communication is nonverbal. It's *how* you articulate things that matters, not what you articulate. You make decisions daily based on your level of self-esteem, and your self-esteem is exhibited to your superiors and peers as self-confident behavior. Others are influenced by your body language, facial gestures, and tonality, things that might tell a different story than your words. You've heard that actions speak louder than words, and it's true: others are influenced and react by reading your nonverbal communication and behavior.

THE BELIEFS THAT ARE CARRIED AROUND WITH YOU ABOUT YOURSELF ARE DERIVED FROM OTHER SOURCES. HOW DO YOU FEEL ABOUT THE SOURCES FROM WHICH YOUR BELIEFS WERE DERIVED? THINK ABOUT HOW THOSE BELIEFS ARE IMPACTING YOU TODAY.

We've already looked at the importance of your childhood experiences in developing adult characteristics. Your parental and peer influences shape your level of self-esteem as a child and during your early adolescent years. Did people tell you that you were beautiful or handsome as a child? Did they compare your intellect to that of your older sibling's, and note that you didn't quite measure up? Did you ever hear your parents say, "Leslie is so smart, but Ryan just isn't applying himself"? Or maybe you heard "Carmen's teeth are so pretty and straight, but Belinda's are very crooked." Often it's these sorts of comments from years past that still allow your negative self to overshadow your opinion of yourself, affect your belief patterns about yourself, and influence your opinions and conclusions.

As you were growing up, you bought into negative feedback without realizing it. Most of this negative feedback originated from others you may have little or no respect for, and today, as an adult, perhaps you'd brush their negative comments aside without a second thought. Yet you still carry the damage done by others to your self-esteem at a very early age. Did you ever stop to think that those people who battered your self-esteem and self-worth may have had low self-esteem themselves?

Now, try to accurately judge feedback from those you respect. It presents a vital opportunity to reshape your self-esteem, deepening your self-understanding and expanding your self-image in the process. You'll be able to see where you need to make a change and where you don't. Low self-esteem and the voice of the negative self give you an inaccurate and incomplete picture of yourself. It's quite possible that you're striving to be better, or actually excelling!

Try this exercise to help boost your self-esteem and stop the voices of the negative self from taking over. Set small goals. Identify your real weakness and strengths in your career and personal life, and develop your professional and interpersonal skills. The process will give confidence boost to you and raise your self-esteem.

―◆―

WERE YOUR CHILDHOOD INTERACTIONS POSITIVELY
ENCOURAGING, OR DO YOU HAVE NEGATIVE THOUGHTS?

―◆―

What Is the Negative Self?

The negative self encompasses feelings, thoughts, and actions that keep you from embracing change. We've seen that it often appears on the heels of success as well. This self-critical voice puts your past failures under a microscope and ignores the positive results. It sets impossible standards of perfection, causing you to assume that other people view you in a negative light.

Think about the relationship between your feelings, your thoughts, and your actions. Have you ever thought even before you started a task, *I can't do this. It's too difficult. I'm stupid. Why did I even think that I could attempt to accomplish this? What an idiot!*

The negative self allows negative thinking to interfere in your life. Sadness, anger, and hurt emerge as warning signals that these are feelings you need to uncover, acknowledge, release, and resolve with as much specificity as possible. If the negative self takes root, you're more likely to avoid new situations, withdraw from people, act on your hostility, and point fingers at others or show sarcasm, all of which steer you away from success. Think of a time when you were transferred to a new department. Did you have feelings of anxiety or anger? Perhaps you blamed other people for your missteps. Or maybe you avoided your colleagues and didn't make an effort to get to know them.

As you prepare to make a presentation in front of a new audience, are you thinking, *I'm going to nail this presentation. They'll love me!* or are you worrying, *I can't do this and I don't even know why I'm trying. They're going to hate me. I'm going to look like an idiot*? If you're thinking about looking like an idiot, more than likely you won't put forth a good effort. This may temporarily relieve your anxiety, but you will not be striving. Instead you will be holding to the status quo—remaining stagnant—and eventually you'll regret your decision. Let's call this your *critical voice*. In a backwards kind of way, your critical voice protects you from your fear of rejection and failure. Your negative self allows negative thinking to become automatic. You may end up living your life with a negatively ingrained self-image and negative thinking that may become routine at an unconscious level.

IDENTIFY THE MESSAGES THAT RUN LIKE A CONSTANT MONOLOGUE INSIDE YOUR HEAD, CAUSING DISRUPTIVE FEELINGS. HOW HAVE YOU DEALT WITH THESE FEELINGS IN THE PAST?

The Carrot or the Whip: Learning How to Choose Reward Instead of Punishment

All of us have negative images that push us towards choosing punishment over reward. Focusing and identifying these images are key steps towards minimizing them. Emma needs to understand just what is contributing to her destructive and maladaptive workplace behavior. As long as she sees the problem as someone else's problem, she will be unable to accomplish this task. She must interact with another human being who can see clearly what she cannot.

Identify and focus clearly on the negative images that are running in your head. Begin to come to terms with these images. Then go to one or more of the roadblock-removing solutions: coaching, mentoring, or psychotherapy. It's like turning on the light when a child is fearful of the dark. If the terror and fear persists in the light, you have to resolve the problem at another level. So, too, for disruptive messages and images that maintain their potency once they're out in the open.

Emma T., the Distorted Reflection

Emma T. is a forty-six-year old Latina from Louisiana with an MBA; she is a senior manager of procurement. She has worked for a Fortune 100 global organization for over eighteen years. A driven individual who will stop at nothing to meet her goals and realize her dreams, she is known as a collaborative manager, but a highly political one.

At the age of sixteen, Emma's mother became pregnant, but Emma's biological father refused to marry her. Emma and her biological father didn't have a relationship with one another until she turned sixteen, and she was never able to fully interact with him. Eventually, her mother married and both Emma's mom and stepfather went on to earn college degrees. Emma herself attended a private high school on a full scholarship and graduated from a prestigious university.

Emma begins to find that she's straying away from other career women in her organization. As she moves through the corporate ranks, her employer asks her to mentor persons of color, share her success with them, and help them gain strategies and skills for advancement. Like Savannah H., Emma is usually "too busy" to help these women and often refers them to other possible mentors. To date she hasn't mentored a Latina or Black woman; she doesn't think she can help them. Emma states, "Many of them are not serious about learning and aren't worth the time." She doesn't help Latina women obtain interviews or advancement within her organization because she "just hasn't had the opportunity to meet a worthy candidate."

Not understanding why she is beginning to have the reputation and label among her peers as the "woman who doesn't like what she sees in the mirror," she's baffled. Even her superiors and direct reports are noticing that Emma never assigns highly visible projects to anyone except Caucasian males. Emma doesn't understand why her colleagues are beginning to inquire about her inability to "find the right candidate of color" despite numerous recommendations from senior executives. She simply responds, "You don't understand. I must find a candidate that is trustworthy. These candidates lack that characteristic."

As Emma and her mother sit and talk one day over cocktails, she begins to discuss her six broken engagements and ponder as to why she has never been able to remain in a stable relationship. A beautiful woman externally, Emma truly doesn't like what she sees in the mirror and wants to understand her anger and indifference relating to other women who have similar ethnicity. She must find answers before her life and career go down the drain.

In the insecurity about her early upbringing, including the true identity of her father, Emma has embraced pejoratives and societal definitions pertaining to people of color—in this instance, Blacks and Latinos. Because of that, Emma was prone to developing a negative self that grew and flourished with the addition of social biases. It is a special problem of people of color that pejorative views aid in developing the negative self. To some extent, Emma can't help herself. She needs interaction with another human being to get beyond the grasp of the negative self. Because Emma's mother is part of her developmental history, it is difficult for Emma not to see her as part of the problem. She'll have to get help from another source—a coach, mentor, or therapist. Which do you think would help Emma most?

You Recognize Them, Do They Recognize You? Revisiting your Family
Francis P., Wishing He Knew Then What He Knows Now

Francis P. is a thirty-two-year-old Caucasian born in the Midwest to prominent upper-class parents. He is a manager of corporate communications employed in a multinational automotive corporation. His father is a scientist and his mother is a college professor, both highly respected members of the community and very active politically.

Francis was the eldest of four children in a home with very strict rules and regulations regarding quality education and family loyalty—both being synonymous with strong beliefs in faith and religion. He majored in banking and finance at a highly regarded university, made excellent grades, and worked hard towards building a solid future for himself.

Unexpectedly, Francis's parents divorced when he was twenty-eight and he saw less and less of his father, who remarried and started a new family. During a holiday weekend, Francis was about to go out on a date with one of his lifelong friends when his mother became frantic. She telephoned his father, explained her concerns, and asked him to come over as soon as possible.

The parents sat Francis down and broke the news that the man he grew up knowing as his father was actually his stepfather, and the young woman Francis was about to go out with was actually his sister. Francis felt shocked and betrayed by his so-called parents, who then set up a meeting between Francis and his biological father—the nice man he always referred to as a wonderful neighbor. Fortunately for Francis, his biological father loved him over the years from a distance, and always treated him with respect. Yet Francis now considers himself an outsider in the family. Suddenly he doesn't know who he really is or where he really belongs. How can he continue on a particular life path and be successful in life?

His father understands his confusion and hurt and explains that people present themselves in different ways in an attempt to find a workable image when they are trying to "find" themselves. "But," he continues, "the only way to truly be successful is to dig deep down to find the authentic *you* within yourself."

The two discover they shared an interest in golf. "There are a lot of different ways to play a particular hole," his father said. "You have to understand what works best for you. You play the hole based on your strengths. In order to improve your game you may get an instructor to help you. The downside of this is that often the instructor begins to change your natural swing. You end up trying to change what used to be natural."

Over time Francis begins to change. He is no longer the outgoing, confident man he once was. At work, he questions his decisions. He wonders what his stepfather or biological father would have done. He starts to identify with others who have stepparents, half sisters, and half brothers. Now Francis is more secretive. There is a dark past that he is uncomfortable sharing with even his closest friends—and, to some degree, even family members. He refrains from joining in conversations and discussions about past family gatherings. Francis the extrovert is now an introvert who wonders, *How many other people are like me, with dark family secrets?* He feels ashamed and less normal. Other people's opinions about Francis are important to him. This unveiled secret has rocked Francis in his home life, social life, and his work life.

Francis's superiors and peers consider him a leader with a bright future ahead. However, this family revelation exposes his self-doubt and lack of confidence, making him relatively withdrawn and requiring him to force himself to be productive. This works only to a point. He takes all photographs of his family out of his office and makes excuses for removing them. His superiors see a difference in his demeanor and quality of work, and have become very concerned. Finally, they suggest that he take a few weeks off to sort through his issues.

Francis does so and then returns to work, hoping that the time off has put some pep in his step, but he is wrong. Now more than ever the demons of his past confront him: his negative self appears and begins to sabotage his ability to make sound decisions. He is responsible for leading team projects, but falls short just as he is about to be successful. Team members take up the slack and save the day, but his shining star is fading. Everyone can see the downward spiral. The once collaborative leader is now a reactive manager who no longer has that zest for work or hunger to defeat life's challenges. He has lost what he thought was his authentic self.

Goals and aspirations develop over time and carry significant traces of your family and heritage. You need to know in which areas your own childhood and family experiences may be producing conflict with a life course appropriate for you now. Do not be surprised if—in your struggle to realign poorly fitting labels, align your actions with the values of your core self, and in essence occupy a new space—your family not so subtly reapplies old labels and discourages action. Remember Jimmy C., the fighting Irishman? When he was finally able to assert himself, he found that the whole family dynamic had shifted.

Getting Beyond the Negative Self

In order to get past the negative self and negative self-talk, you have to slow down, take a deep breath, and give yourself permission to reaffirm daily who you are and what you strive to be. When it's crunch time and you think, *This is a disaster! I'll never get this finished on time!* what you're telling yourself is that this task can't be accomplished and you're doomed. Instead, try thinking, *How can I get this project finished on time? What will help me do it?* You're now telling yourself that your task will be completed and your project will be finished on time. How about the familiar cry, *There's no way that I can meet my sales quota for the month!* Again, you're telling yourself you can't possibly reach your goal. Instead try, *What strategies can I incorporate that will help me quickly reach my quota and blow my numbers out of the water?* Not that we're trying to oversimplify things, but if you change what you say to yourself and how you say it, you can begin to take baby steps toward freeing yourself from the voices of the negative self.

DO YOU ENGAGE IN NEGATIVE SELF-TALK? WHAT DO SOME
OF THESE CONVERSATIONS SOUND LIKE? HOW ARE THEY
IMPACTING YOU IN YOUR CAREER AND LIFE?

It takes time to get past the negativity that you experienced as a child and then dragged into your adult life, as well as the negativity that you experience now as an adult. Get in tune with yourself and do what makes you happy. Oftentimes when you're plagued with low self-esteem, you can't " you tend to disregard or even demean the things that make you happy.

Next, stay away from people who don't have your best interests at heart, the demeaning types who play on your weaknesses instead of your strengths. Many of the people who undermine you and make you feel small *feel small themselves* (and have low self-esteem). Develop friendships with people you trust and respect, and who will have honest dialogue with you about your strengths and will help you work through your challenges or weaknesses.

Get busy living your life with purpose and passion. True happiness comes from the inside, and if you're busy being happy, you have less time for negative self-talk, low self-esteem, and the negative self.

Imagine sitting with colleagues who are talking about their accomplishments and beginning to feel a little intimidated and self-conscious by their high level of confidence. You excuse yourself and retreat, making up excuses that keep you away from them. Pay attention to your feelings, behaviors, and actions. Among those people who appear to dispositively size you up in a matter of seconds, there are those who appreciate honesty about feelings. Those are the people you want in your corner. There are many people around you right now who have the same problem that you're suffering from. Instead of excusing yourself and getting away from your colleagues, take a chance on being honest and open. You'll be more respected for your sincerity and honesty if you say, "You know what, I'm feeling a bit uncomfortable right now." That's better than being the person who displays a false bravado that people can see through.

> DO YOU SURROUND YOURSELF WITH SUPPORTIVE AND POSITIVE PEOPLE, OR DO YOU HAVE PEOPLE WHO UNDERMINE YOU AND DRAG YOU DOWN RATHER THAN PICK YOU UP? ARE YOU A SUPPORT TO OTHERS? HOW IS THIS DYNAMIC IMPACTING YOUR CAREER AND PERSONAL LIFE?

Remember the Soup Nazi on the television show *"Seinfeld"* who, if patrons stepped out of line, would get angry and say, "No soup for you"? You want to think like that too: "no soup" for anyone who brings negativity into your life. Take care of yourself by only having people around you who want to help you move forward in your career and life—those who will give you positive reinforcement. Listen to people as they respond to your discomfort. Do they say, "That's okay, we can talk about that later. Let's move on to another subject?" Such a response might mean that you didn't have anything to fear in the first place. However, if their response is to ignore you and continue talking, then they may be hiding their own low self-esteem behind false bravado.

Take a step back, stay in the moment, listen to others, and you'll soon realize that you're not focusing on your lack of confidence. You'll receive positive reinforcement and feedback from others because they'll appreciate your focused attention on them. As your self-esteem grows and the voices of the negative self dissipate, you'll find that you're no longer inhibited or intimidated by the confidence of others. Rather, you'll begin to enjoy and appreciate their confidence—and they yours.

As the negative self shrinks, the likelihood of failure shrinks along with it. Once you've yanked up those deeply rooted negative feelings—on your own or, more probably, with outside help—the prospects for failure in the future become dim indeed, and the promise of success shines brightly in the distance.

> THINK ABOUT A TIME WHEN YOU WERE UNCOMFORTABLE WITH A SITUATION? WERE YOU OPEN AND HONEST WITH OTHERS ABOUT YOUR FEELINGS? HOW DID PEOPLE REACT TO YOU?

Action Items
- Define success and failure for yourself.
- Reflect on your experiences after attaining success and experiencing failure.
- Uncover and address the conflict you experience.
- Have a positive conversation with yourself.
- Honor and celebrate your accomplishments, no matter how big or small.

Chapter 8: Women: Getting Over the "Little Lady" Syndrome

I am always doing that which I cannot do, in order that I may learn how to do it.

—Pablo Picasso, Spanish painter and sculptor (1881–1973)

Women face special challenges in learning to purposively strive and to achieve success in their careers and lives. They encounter different hurdles in the corporate world from the ones men have to deal with, and now we'll look more closely at some of these gender-specific issues. (In the next chapter, we'll give the men their turn.) Women may have personal labels, negative selves, and childhood influences that have certain characteristics in common. Recognizing and understanding those characteristics, and knowing how to respond, helps both women and men better understand what makes women successful in the business world and how they can be helped to reach their full potential.

Most of the difficulty women have in taking advantage of emerging opportunities comes from internalized labels that fit society's approved definitions of them, but at the same time sharply limit their aspirations and accomplishments. First among these is the "little lady" syndrome. Girls grow up in little-lady boxes, which lead to grown-lady boxes containing traditionally circumscribed roles, such as wife, mother, housekeeper, and chief cook (though not the chef) and bottle washer.

Then there's the stereotypic portrayal of women as the epitome of quiet and selfless strength: long-suffering motherly types with limited individual needs. Too many contemporary women find themselves feeling they have to assume this mantle of strength and function as the idealized strong woman whether that role fits them or not.

ARE YOU ATHLETIC, OR DO YOU HAVE A FRIEND WHO IS ATHLETIC OR TOMBOYISH? HOW DO YOU REACT TO HER? WHAT EXPERIENCES HAVE YOU HAD IF YOU'VE BEEN VIEWED AS A TOMBOY?

Until recently, there had also been a tomboy box, which didn't entitle women to any particular status, but relegated girls to being thought odd or having questionable sexual orientation and being less feminine. Fortunately, today the concept of athleticism has somewhat superseded this type of thinking, though athletic girls and women still find themselves having to defend their femininity to some degree. In the 1920s and '30s, when gold metal Olympians Gertrude Ederle (who was also the first woman to swim the English Channel) and Babe Didrikson (later a golf celebrity) were making headlines, athletic women were treated far differently than they are today. Even in 1948, when Dutch runner Fanny Blankers-Koen won four gold medals at the Olympic Games as a mother of two, the press called her "the flying housewife." Some of you may remember the great tennis star Billie Jean King, who struck a blow for women everywhere when, in 1973, she defeated aging tennis star Bobby Riggs at the Houston Astrodome after Riggs (who was fifty-five at the time) had made an open challenge to women players. Today women athletes have earned an encouraging measure of celebrity and respect.

There's no doubt that women of all types garner far more respect in the workplace now than they did in Gertrude Ederle's day, but their gender still labels and limits them in ways they need to be aware of in order to survive and thrive.

Overcoming the Restricting Images of the Past
Beth and the "Little Lady"

You remember Beth, our well-regarded overachiever who seems determined to make failure out of success. Beth is suffering from little lady syndrome. In fact, she's a classic case of this distinctively feminine form of negative self. Beth's mother taught her that a woman's role is to be attractive, refined, and perpetually auditioning for the ultimate role as "a great man's lady." Beth needs to listen less ambivalently to the voice of her father, who encouraged her to seek respect from her colleagues and go as far as she could in the business world.

But Beth feels the lack of attention, resources, and respect. (My research shows she has plenty of company.) Beth has been an advocate of her team and direct reports and ensures that they get all of the tools necessary to run a department successfully. This implies that her company supports Beth, but her negative self prevents her from seeing and believing that.

At some point, most women face the norms of tradition, which impose labels and limits associated with society's definitions of what a "good girl" and a "good woman" should be. A negative self develops, representing the inner voice that reminds a woman when she's behaving or thinking outside of the little-lady box or the strong motherly stereotype. The biggest obstacle to the achievement of women resides in the little-lady aspect of the negative self.

Taylor E., the Angry Lady

Taylor E. is a bright, thirty-six-year-old human resources manager at a Fortune 200 company. From her cheerleading days in high school through her partying days at a state college to today, Taylor was always the chipper one. Although she feels that label is incorrect, she feels obligated to act cheerful no matter how she really feels.

Finally even the appearance of cheerfulness disappears. After two years without advancing to the director or executive level, Taylor often appears angry and seems resentful of others' advancement. Her HR coaching sessions with executives, formerly her favorite part of work, are increasingly difficult. Taylor receives her first negative performance evaluation. At her husband's suggestion Taylor asks for a mentor, and management assigns her a male executive to help he achieve her goals in the organization.

Taylor's mentor helps her understand that she feels burdened by the cheerful label she grew up with, and that she relied on it to define herself. As she grows older and the demands of work become more substantively difficult, her superiors don't perceive enough depth or substance in Taylor to do the more senior jobs. Though she is excited about the mentoring process at first, it soon grows stale. She blames her mentor for her problems and doesn't feel that he is acknowledging her many gifts and talents. Taylor asks to be reassigned to a different mentor, preferably a female, but the company denies her request.

HAVE YOU EVER BEEN MENTORED BY ANYONE IN YOUR WORKPLACE? DO YOU PREFER ONE GENDER OVER ANOTHER FOR YOUR MENTOR? IF SO, WHY?

Taylor becomes angrier with each successive rejection. She feels picked on, and notices she's excluded from important meetings. Taylor ultimately becomes a maverick, doing everything to buck the system instead of following the advice of her mentor. Taylor feels that her organization is partly responsible for her failure. Is she in fact the problem, or does her organization owe it to her to listen to her concerns about her mentor?

Let's focus on mentoring as a solution for Taylor. We've seen that mentoring is a powerful method for helping you get rid of old thought patterns and behaviors, and clean out that label box of all the destructive labels that feed the negative self and encourage the status quo. What's significant to us in Taylor's story is that there are special permutations of the negative self and distinctive aspects of mentoring to women.

The classic novel *Gone With the Wind* gives us two vivid examples of negative labels for women. The first, represented by the slave nursemaid and confidante Mammy, embodies images of matriarchal strength and caring, a strong, sacrificial, self-denying presence. Then there's Scarlett O'Hara, the ultimate Southern little lady, exemplifying the dysfunctional socialized self. That is, it is dysfunctional in the context of historical change in not allowing the self to accept new opportunities.

> THINK ABOUT YOUR FAMILY TIES AND YOUR WORKPLACE. ARE YOU A REBEL AND A CHANGE AGENT, OR ARE YOU A TRADITIONALIST WHO IS COMFORTABLE KEEPING THINGS JUST THE WAY THEY ARE? HOW HAS THAT BEHAVIOR HELPED OR HINDERED YOUR CAREER?

Two conflicting female personalities come together in the 2004 Broadway play *Caroline, or Change*. The central character of the play is a strong Black woman providing for herself and family in the context of a changing but still bigoted South. Her work for a liberal Northern family living in Louisiana allows her to see the "promised land" of true equality, but Caroline's strengths are built upon pushing back safely against the mores and strictures of that Jim Crow South. Caroline can't rebel. Her daughter proves to be the true rebel. And though unsympathetic at first, repudiating some of Caroline's actions and in many ways neutralizing her strength and effectiveness in protecting her family, we learn to respect her. Toward the play's end we perceive clearly that the hope for change lies within the daughter, who not only can see the promised land, but who understands that entering into it depends on rupturing many of the ambivalent and destructive ties in that society that Caroline protects.

> HAVE YOU EXPERIENCED THE LITTLE-LADY SYNDROME IN THE WORKPLACE? HOW HAS THAT IMPACTED YOUR SELF-ESTEEM AND CAREER?

The ideal mentoring relationship is a mutual choice by two individuals in pursuit of a particular, specified goal, though as Taylor's experience teaches us, the ideal mentor doesn't always materialize. The negative self—as well as the dysfunctional elaboration of the socialized or status quo self—is an obstacle to "becoming" and represents a pattern and boundary that mentoring must cross if the mentoring process is to be successful.

The most successful women in the corporate world often have multiple mentors over the course of their careers. My research revealed that women managers and executives received a greater number of promotions based on how many mentors they had. Those with several mentors were promoted at a rate of 70 percent, compared to 50 percent without multiple mentors.

The Mentoring Dyad: Characteristics and Pitfalls

Mentoring is the ideal solution for overcoming the particular aspirational barrier that the little lady represents. Throughout your career and personal life you can have many mentors helping you attain your goals. But first you must get far enough beyond the grasp of the negative self to be able to listen and learn—and the responsibility for this first step lies with you as the protégé. Insistence on working with people of your own gender and/or ethnicity, and of your own age bracket may be a manifestation of the little-lady syndrome. While women mentoring women seems a natural—and may, in fact, work better than the alternative—one of the inherent dangers of the system is having mentor and protégé huddling together in the same foxhole under siege.

> IF YOU'VE PARTICIPATED IN A MENTOR/PROTÉGÉ DYAD WITH A PERSON OF A DIFFERENT RACE, THINK ABOUT YOUR EXPERIENCE. HOW DID IT IMPACT YOUR CAREER DEVELOPMENT? WERE YOU OPEN TO THE EXPERIENCE AND DID YOU FEEL THAT IT BENEFITED YOU?

This may happen if mentor and protégé identify with each other too closely, and it will hamper or completely prevent the kind of broad interaction characteristic of successful mentoring relationships. On the other hand, mentor and protégé may lock into a static situation where the mentor resists the growth of the protégé or the protégé resists giving up a dependant posture in relation to the mentor.

Is It an Issue of Gender, Age, or Race?

In looking at the literature available on women in the workplace, I recognized a particular lack of information about women of color. Since these workers deal every day with two of the three elephants of gender, race, and age discrimination, their experiences with and views about mentoring and related issues give them a unique perspective.

The purpose of sharing this information with you is to shine a light on specific issues that impact employees based on both gender and race. Knowledge about these issues can create an opportunity for awareness, understanding, and forward thinking for you as individuals and organizational leaders who wish to attract, retain, and develop the best talent in this global community. Because this research covers ground that relatively few other studies have addressed, we'll present the results more fully than we have for other points in our discussion.

I addressed head-on, both empirically and qualitatively, the issues of race and gender that employees face in the corporate arena. During a focus group, ten Black female middle managers and senior level executives discussed why both gender and race mattered in choosing and being chosen as a mentor. The participants shared their views by answering three poignant questions about their workplace experiences. The average age of participants was 42 and the average combined household income was over $150,000 annually. On average, the group had a master's level education and nine years working for the present employer. A majority of the participants worked in Fortune 500 high tech entities employing between 5,000 and 100,000 persons. A majority of the participants also felt passed over for promotions. Most had received one or no promotions within the last five years.

Statement One

I asked research participants to respond to three questions or statements relating to mentoring. The first: *There is (has been) a Caucasian female who has served as my mentor in my work environment; and there is (has been) a Black female who has served as my mentor in my work environment.*

Women, more often than not, were able to answer affirmatively to these statements. Perhaps you are more comfortable being mentored by someone who looks like you; however, if you are of color, it is more likely that someone of a different race than your own will mentor you, and you may have a more difficult time either finding or being a mentor and developing a successful mentor/protégé relationship. Barriers to advancement for the women in the study included a lack of mentoring. Some select comments follow.

- Director of corporate relations, age 37

   We need persons to mentor us at a higher level. We also need to be more visible, and have access to senior management. If senior management believes in you, you can write your own ticket to some extent, and I'm not just seeing that in this organization. I am alone.

Support from other Blacks and other women were a major theme that several subjects expressed.

- Program manager, age 42

   We must partner with our Caucasian female counterparts and obtain their support whenever possible. In essence, have them as allies. Now what I am doing is being proactive and seeking out a mentor above me who is either a Caucasian male or female . . . I believe that we are barriers to our advancement in a sense because of many reasons: we want to be with our families, we don't seek out support and be proactive (we are mainly reactive), and finally, we are too complacent at times. We get comfortable with our paychecks and we don't try to learn as much as possible about other departments and other functions.

- Senior buyer, age 40

   It's a combination of things that keep us from advancing. We as Black women have our own separate set of issues that we bring into the organization, and I don't think that we are ready to deal with those issues and neither is the organization.

Another participant gave a concrete example of a situation that illustrated a lack of support of others of her own ethnicity, and summarized what women need to overcome this problem.

- Executive director, age 46

   In a nutshell, we keep ourselves from advancing because we don't advance or give others a chance who are like us. We need good mentors, good relationships with powerful people (no matter what color they are), and we need to help bring in other people of color to prove to the Caucasian establishment that we are good, educated, and professional workers who are worthy of advancement.

Participants' perception and experience of being a mentor generally were not positive. Protégés were not respectful, did not believe in mentorship by Black women, and felt that it would not be helpful in their advancement, as indicated by these comments.

- Senior buyer, age 40

    What I am seeing is that people feel more comfortable with people who look and act like them or mirror them. They don't want to take the time to get to know others who are different . . . people don't feel comfortable with people of a different gender from theirs. So it's a double-edged sword . . . Now, if you couple those issues with having to mentor others who don't necessarily want to be mentored by you, that raises even more frustration. It's an uphill battle.

Participants articulated an issue relating to gender as well. Men were uncomfortable being mentored by women. Men tended to have issues surrounding female mentorship, as noted here.

- Program manager, age 42

    I think that when I have to mentor men they have a problem with that. I have been assigned to mentor women who have been okay with it, so not only is it a race issue, but it is a gender issue as well. Some men have asked to be reassigned to another mentor, and you look around, and they're with another male.

Caucasian women who were mentored by Black women tended to be uncomfortable as well.

- Program manager, age 41

    I mentored a Caucasian female and an Asian female at the same time . . . These two women were close friends, and they both asked for another mentor. People need to understand that when they ask to be reassigned, it makes the mentor look bad, and this can ultimately be harmful.

Focus group participants stated that they have a fear of being judged as protégés, as well.

• Senior engineer, age 38

This experience has made me leery of being mentored for two reasons: I'm afraid of what my mentors will think of me in the initial stages and in the long-term. I don't know if they are mentoring me because they feel obligated or because they really want to help. Secondly, my fear is that I will be judged negatively if I don't learn quickly, and they may hurt my career in the long-term. You just never know who is talking to whom, and what is being said behind my back.

Some participants believed that Black superiors did not approach them and offer their assistance as a mentor.

Mentorship Based on Race
Mentorship by Caucasians has been a mixed experience as well.

• Senior engineer, age 38

I have noticed that the women are a bit apprehensive and don't fully offer their support. Only two Caucasian men over my career have been my mentors, and they have been wonderful.

• Senior buyer, age 40

As far as being a mentee, I have had a very good Caucasian female mentor who has been very supportive throughout the years. She is now retired, but I still call her from time to time and get her opinion about issues . . . I do feel that being mentored by her helped me to advance eventually.

Question Two

This question elicited some interesting responses from women of color. *How did you receive your position within your organization and what do you believe contributed to your being hired?*

- Executive director, age 45

    Through networking, being mentored, due to my education, experience, and contacts with influential people.

- Senior engineer, age 47

    I aligned myself with the personality/work style of the hiring manager who was a Caucasian female. My experience and skill set also helped.

Question Three

It is important to note that women (and men) agreed that mentoring, job performance, fitting within the corporate culture, and access to influential people were the keys to advancement and success in their careers. Here are several responses from women of color to the third question: *What do you believe is most important or key to advancement within your organization?*

- Training manager, age 38

    Being mentored and also networking with everyone and anyone because that may be the next job opening in your area of interest.

- Regional VP, age 48

    I think hard work and willingness to be a team player are key . . . meeting the right people and having opportunities to work for those people (to show them what you can do) is critical . . . showing an interest in the organization is also very important (i.e., learning the function of other departments or looking for ways to make the organization better)

- Senior analyst, age 47

The corporate culture is such that it gives free reign to overseas subsidiaries to develop their own culture. Within each subsidiary, this is repeated at the departmental level, so advancement within a particular department depends a great deal on the culture and management style of that department. My advancements have been due to building relationships with the right people and using those relationships to lobby for my cause. Without the ability to champion this task, I would not have advanced to this level.

Responses from Caucasian women were similar.

- Program manager, age 48

Having the ability to manage upward. Being seen as someone who can fit within a more exclusive culture.

- Project engineer, age 46

Technical knowledge and my ability to make sound decisions. Establishing the right relationships with people who can help me advance. Knowing my job and doing it well.

- Vice president, age 49

Performance is key. Organizations need leaders and people who do not sit and wait for things to happen; they look for people who make things happen. Also, having shared values with the senior executives of the organization along with being very vocal about my career goals, making myself visible, and taking on more responsibility.

In summary, these participants strongly agreed that certain conditions affected their ability to succeed in the workplace: appropriate attention, access to influential people, the degree of support and respect from Caucasians and non-Caucasians, stereotypes, language used in defining Black women (i.e., the use of phrases such as *women and minorities*), gender discrimination, and being considered a person of lesser caliber than Caucasians, Asians and Indians.

These women further agreed that while mentoring is important, Black women don't feel that they can take advantage of mentorship or be valued mentors due to the lack of respect and fear of being judged as an incompetent mentor or protégé. The lack of respect and attention seems based on stereotypical responses to Black women from their superiors and peers, and the recognition from subordinates that a power structure exists within organizations, which is where the lack of attention and respect in relationship to mentoring exists. If a Black woman feels disrespected, her subordinates will hear about it, creating an environment that discourages others from mentoring by this race of women. Subordinates will come not to accept Black women as mentors because they see that senior people in the organization don't show them respect. This lack of respect originates from stereotypes surrounding both race and gender, and the inability for parties to discuss openly the issue of race and gender difference.

The Glass and Concrete Ceilings

The struggle continues for leaders who happen to be women; they must wade through a sea of stereotypes to rise to the top of their professions. They often work under glass ceilings, watching what goes on at the top but never reaching the pinnacle themselves. Women of color often find themselves under surrounded by a concrete ceiling, as revealed in my research. Sometimes a woman might break the glass ceiling, but a concrete ceiling is solid and impenetrable.

Research participants were asked the questions, *Do you feel that there is a glass ceiling present in your organization? Do you feel there is a concrete ceiling present in your organization?* What emerged was that women were significantly more likely than men to perceive an existence of a glass ceiling, but not a concrete ceiling. Women of color, specifically Black women, were significantly more likely than Caucasian women to perceive a concrete ceiling, with a trend toward women of color, specifically Black women, being more likely to perceive a glass ceiling as well.

When perceptions of the concrete ceiling were examined by race and by gender separately, gender differences in the perception of the glass ceiling and racial differences in the perception of the concrete ceiling emerged, with a trend toward Blacks (both men and women) perceiving *both* as existent in their workplace. This finding is quite significant and reveals the fact that although women experience some of the same barriers to career advancement, women of color, specifically Black women, have unique barriers that impact long-term sustained career success.

Coping Strategies

The critical role of mentoring coupled with emotional adaptive skills that may assist in the process of business success must be understood. One clinical and organizational psychological strategy most often employed is coping. Development of effective coping methods became essential for maintenance of psychological symmetry, problem solving, goal attainment, and actualization. The definition of coping as "behavior in response to a problem" is useful, and refers to your effort to master conditions of threat, harm, or challenge that you perceive, and that result from a problem women have identified.

> HOW ARE YOU "COPING"? HAS YOUR METHOD OF COPING
> HELPED YOUR CAREER OR HINDERED IT?

Barriers to Women's Advancement

Barriers to career progression for women are subtle and deeply entrenched. These barriers fall into three categories: 1) individual level, 2) group level, and 3) organizational level. Each barrier contains complex forces, both visible and invisible, public and private events, stable and changing relations. Barriers to advancement are both interrelated and cyclical in nature. Presenting barriers in this form allows us to look closely at the systematic interconnectedness between and within groups of barriers. The influence of barriers may not be a one-time occurrence in your life, but rather a challenge you experience throughout various stages of your career.

> WHAT ARE YOU DOING TO OVERCOME THE BARRIERS THAT
> BLOCK FROM MOVING FORWARD IN YOUR CAREER?

Individual-Level Barriers

Issues impacting your psychological and social well-being appear at this level. These are the barriers embedded in your psychological make-up, roles in the organization, interpersonal style and conflict management, values, attitudes, goals, and self-identity. Individual level barriers include: 1) subtle racism and prejudice, 2) managing duality and bicultural stress, 3) self-limiting behavior, and 4) tokenism and presumed incompetence. It is important to note that these barriers impact all women, but particularly women of color.

Subtle Racism and Prejudice
Subtle racism and prejudice are considered to be the most menacing and tenacious barrier at the individual level, with implications that are the strongest for both the group and organizational level as well. Subtle racism and prejudice occur through indirectness and avoidance, which is behavior that is difficult to eradicate. In the workplace, if you're the one who draws the conclusion that racism and prejudice exist, oftentimes you may be seen as too touchy or too sensitive or unrealistic about the issue; someone with a chip on her shoulder, or someone who just doesn't fit in. Unlike racial hostility or overt bigotry, subtle racism is hidden below the surface. Due to its covert nature, the psychological damage to you can be far greater because this modern form of racism and prejudice is often not apparent to the perpetrators and isn't easily acknowledged or addressed. The end result is these behaviors and beliefs are reproduced, seep into everyday life, and become deeply entrenched.

Managing Bicultural Stress and Cultural Duality
The key issue for you here is the ability to fit into your organization's corporate culture, but it must be in concert with who you are; therefore, you're walking a very fine line and must be master of rather than slave to that culture.

Self-Limiting Behavior
Self-limiting behavior is a two-dimensional offshoot of the psychological phenomenon of biculturality and managing dual cultural contexts. Self-limiting behavior can be detrimental to your career if you lack organizational savvy. It is important not to limit yourself by being strategic in your career development, knowing your colleagues' agendas, paying close attention to organizational politics, and paying close attention to the agenda of your colleagues and bosses.

HAVE YOU EXPERIENCED SELF-LIMITING BEHAVIOR OR TOKENISM IN YOUR CAREER? HOW ARE YOU HANDLING THESE ISSUES, AND WHAT ARE YOU DOING TO OVERCOME THIS PROBLEM? IS THIS A CAREER ROADBLOCK FOR YOU OR DO YOU FEEL THAT IT'S HELPING YOU IN SOME WAY?

Tokenism and Presumed Incompetence

The final individual-level barrier is tokenism. It isn't clear at present whether a consequence of tokenism for all women is the same. My research provides a useful framework for a variety of negative perceptions of women labeled as tokens. More often than not, tokenism negatively impacts the career aspirations of women of color. This significant barrier appears when women enter a predominantly male organization, before they have the opportunity to establish their competence.

Group-Level Barriers

Group level barriers are significant and include: 1) perceptions of cultural differences and ethnocentrism, and 2) group density. Intergroup cultural differences have been shown to have strong effects on behaviors, attitudes, and interactions among differing genders and races in the workplace. Substantial support of significant differences is evident among racial groups in managing interpersonal conflict, cooperative versus competitive behavior, communication styles, and perceptions of organization experiences.

Perception of Cultural Differences

In both a heterogeneous or homogeneous group, a woman or woman of color, oriented towards more cooperative behavior, may appear incompetent or not having the necessary skills to compete. The findings of my study reveal that low ability and incompetence correlate with more cooperative and conciliatory behavior. The study also revealed communication style differences between the genders and races.

An interdependency exists between all groups of women and the women of color represented in the workplace. Women and women of color form identity groups defined by gender, race, kinship, and class. Some groups you may be born into, and affiliations with these groups are difficult to change. Groups in which you work (organizational groups) may also represent significant reference groups. Clearly these relationships are, relatively speaking, set in stone.

DO YOU FIND YOURSELF BEING THE ONLY WOMAN OR WOMAN OF COLOR IN A GROUP? HAS THIS BEEN A ROADBLOCK FOR YOU? HOW ARE YOU HANDLING THIS SITUATION? ARE YOU BEING PROACTIVE OR REACTIVE?

As a woman, you may have expectations in common with another woman when lumped together in informal networks, and being mutually supportive and dependent on one another for information. When a woman does not conform to such expectations, it may jeopardize her status within the group. If behavior does not conform to group norms, this woman may be isolated by group members and perceived as not being a good group member.

Group Density
The last group-level barrier for women in the workplace is group density in relation to race. Group density refers to the relative percentage of persons of color in a work group. A rather complex relationship exists between the number of women of color in a work group or organization and the treatment a particular may receive.

Organizational or Structural-Level Barriers
The organizational-level barrier occurs around structures, policies, practices, and organizationwide systems. At the organizational level, barriers include: 1) access to mentoring, 2) performance evaluation and promotion processes, 3) functional segregation into staff-type jobs, and 4) downsizing policies. Examples of these are selection and recruitment procedures, development or promotion policies, career-planning systems, performance evaluation methods, and training and development programs.

Mentors, Performance Evaluations, and Promotion Processes
My research shows that there are differing perceptions of how organizational or structural-level barriers can impact you based on both gender and race. For example:

- Black women were more likely than Caucasian men (the reference group) to agree with the statement, There is (has been) a Black female who has served as my mentor in my work environment.

- Black women were more likely than Caucasian men to disagree with the statement, I receive equal respect from Caucasian and non-Caucasian staff members.

- Black women were more likely than Caucasian men to disagree with the statement, I receive appropriate attention (i.e., engaged conversation, respectful tone dialogue, responsiveness to queries) from Caucasian and non-Caucasian staff members.

- Black women were more likely than Caucasian men to agree with the statement, My organization values traditional Caucasian universities in making its promotion choices.

- Black women were more likely than Caucasian men to agree with the statement, Competition among my peers is perceived by my superiors as a positive activity.

- Caucasian women were more likely than Caucasian men to agree with the statements, There is or has been a Caucasian female who has served as a mentor in my work environment, and There is or has been a Black female who has served as a mentor in my work environment.

- Caucasians (both men and women) were more likely to agree that competition among peers was perceived as a negative activity by their superiors. Caucasians were more likely to agree that a Caucasian woman has served as a mentor in their work environment. Caucasians were more likely to agree that they receive equal respect from Caucasian and non-Caucasian staff members.

- Caucasians were more likely to agree that they receive appropriate attention (i.e., engaged conversation, respectful tone dialogue, responsiveness to queries) from Caucasian and non-Caucasian staff members. Caucasians were more likely to agree with the statement, My organization values traditional Caucasian universities in making its promotion choices.

Functional and Occupational Segregation

Women are often placed in functional and occupational segregation into positions not on the pipeline to top management.

Downsizing

The final organizational barrier impacting women, specifically women of color, is downsizing, which is a recent phenomenon. Employees of color have experienced negative effects and consequences of downsizing. Women of color are impacted more than other groups as they're often the last hired and therefore the first to be laid off during corporate restructuring and downsizing. If you, as a woman of color, are selected to remain in the organization, you may be conflicted about motives of management. You may not know if you are a survivor because you're a woman of color, or because you're a good performer.

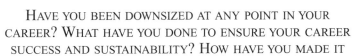

HAVE YOU BEEN DOWNSIZED AT ANY POINT IN YOUR CAREER? WHAT HAVE YOU DONE TO ENSURE YOUR CAREER SUCCESS AND SUSTAINABILITY? HOW HAVE YOU MADE IT KNOWN THAT YOUR SKILLS ARE NEEDED?

The Secrets of Successfully Mentoring Women

Successful mentoring programs for women will likely include these five characteristics:

They identify and practice effective procedures for benchmarking and evaluating the program, specifically targeting women and women of color to ensure that organizational equity in corporate America by enhancing career development strategies, affinity group availability, and participation.

They focus on networking, job performance, corporate culture inclusion, and access to influential people within the corporation. My research showed that women felt gender discrimination, while men reported that their gender empowered them rather than hindered them.

They persuade the organization to match protégé skills with organizational goals and values. When women encounter the notion of "fit" without objective standards, the entire process seems entirely subjective. The research indicates that men do not have this problem.

They address inclusivity, collaboration, and diversity as key components in dealing with gender, race, and age issues.

They affirm that the more familiar a mentor or protégé is with her (or his) own heritage, the easier it will be for her to work within a mentoring program. The program should seek out those with a strong sense of self that serves as a source of strength rather than a potential liability to career advancement.

Are You on the Path to Power?

The struggle continues for leaders who happen to be women. You must struggle through a sea of stereotypes to rise to the top of your profession. But it's possible to break through the glass ceilings and concrete ceilings we're heard frustrated women describe, especially women of color. Women see a glass ceiling far more often than men, and women of color report facing that seemingly impenetrable concrete more often than any other group. But we've seen that with the right strategy, women can break through and find success and fulfillment in their careers and still remain faithful to their true selves.

The right mentoring program is crucial for women as they move up the corporate ladder. And it's also essential that they develop effective coping methods, defined as *behavior in response to a problem*, for maintaining psychological symmetry, solving problems, attaining goals, and actualization.

How are you coping? Has your method of coping helped your career or hindered it?

Coping encompasses your effort to master conditions of threat, harm, or challenge that you perceive, and that result from a problem women have identified.

But after considering all the research, mentoring, and talk of breaking through glass ceilings, what are some of the ways you can tell whether or not you're on the right path? Here are some indications that will help you determine if you're on the path to power.

Line Versus Staff

If you are in a line position, colleagues assume that you have a direct line of control and responsibility from the chief executive office to middle management executives, supervisors, and workers. Companies develop staff positions to meet line executives' needs. If you are in a staff function, you assist the line in performing its tasks. Staff does not retain direct power over line; therefore, there are clear lines of authority encircling the relationship between staff and line. The staff can offer recommendations and suggestions, but staff or functional vice presidents rarely become upwardly mobile and obtain senior executive status. What does this mean to you? The implication is that persons in line positions have the ability to exercise more authority, influence, and power. If you're in a line position, you're probably on the right path.

Formulating Policy

Management's priority and concern is formulating policy. Policy making denotes power. In the corporate environment, many women are not in decision-making roles, which translates into a lack of power. A company may have to change its way of delegating policy making to ensure a place of equity in the society and organizations. Leaders are policy makers; in the right corporate environment, policy making becomes a shared experience and value that can change the face of the world of work and ultimately help to enhance your career.

Operating Budget

Senior executives have the responsibility of managing financial resources. If you're not responsible for an organization's operating budget, you're placed in positions without power, authority, and the ability to make decisions. Having no *resources* to accomplish the goal of changing the power structure in an organization translates into having a position without power and authority.

Kinds of Power

As you travel the pathway to corporate power you'll see that it comes in various forms. You must continue to observe, learn, and refine your understanding of power. This may move you to a more sophisticated level of functioning. Being at ease with the specific language and imagery of power in your organization is imperative for you to remain upwardly mobile in the workplace.

> WHAT KIND OF POWER DO YOU HAVE IN YOUR ORGANIZATION? HOW HAS IT HELPED OR HINDERED YOUR CAREER AND YOUR SELF-ESTEEM?

Associative power stems from your close alignment with someone deemed powerful. Thus, a shadow or halo effect results from the presumption that you speak or act on behalf of some powerful person, and in itself is a form of power.

Charismatic power, sometimes called personal power, has everything to do with the individual. It is that unique combination of intelligence and pleasing traits and characteristics that compels and attracts others. Although others may not know why, they are drawn to this person and want to follow him or her. Charisma can be immediately apparent or only appreciated over time, but once identified is unmistakable.

Power through reward, the opposite of coercive power, is based on your ability to meet or satisfy someone else's need. It is the carrot, the seduction factor, drawing in those who want something from the holder of power.

Coercive power is based on your ability to punish or frustrate another person. This behavior is no longer generally acceptable, so it is seldom overtly used in modern corporations.

Though there are still plenty of discriminatory barriers to overcome, both subtle and overt, women today have more power and more opportunity in the business world than ever before. Their challenge is to take advantage of every opportunity to reinforce their abilities and prove their skills. Men, for their part, must continue moving down the path of enlightenment that recognizes women as equal and full partners in every aspect of the corporate realm. There's no room for assumptions and stereotypes; not only are they unfair—in today's world, they're bad business. This obviously isn't to say that all women fit this pattern any more than all women would rather run in the Olympics or raise children at home (or both). Casting off their negative selves, taking inspiration from the examples of other women, and reaching out to both men and women mentors who can teach and help them, women workers are poised to claim their own special brand of power in the global marketplace.

Action Items
- Uncover your barriers to advancement in your career.
- Be open to mentoring others who are different.

Chapter 9: Men: Winning Over the Warrior King

Try to learn something about everything and everything about something.

—Thomas Henry Huxley, English biologist (1825–1895)

Now we turn from the little-lady box to the "little man" and the cult of the warrior king. Just as women face distinctive challenges on their way to purposive striving and career fulfillment, men have concerns and solutions that are specific to their gender. Men need their own brand of mentoring, particularly in environments where they stand side by side with women in previously unfamiliar environments, such as the chairman's or CEO's office at a multinational corporation, or among professionals such as scientists, physicists, doctors, and lawyers.

Men grow up in little-man boxes where competition and struggle are the underpinning. *Peter Pan*, *Penrod*, and *Lord of the Flies* are literary expressions of this concept. The late analyst and identity researcher Erik Erikson noted that when given blocks, little girls would build block houses or structures with broad and substantial bases, while little boys build spires or towers. According to Erikson, this indicates the basic and intrusive nature of boys. Then there's the testosterone-driven "cult of the warrior," wherein every challenge or confrontation is war and the only rule is death before dishonor. The snarling bad guy, the sullen tough guy, and the taciturn he-man are all graduates of the little-man preschool and the school for the warrior. As the sensitive male has emerged in recent times, the he-man image has remitted to some extent, but is far from gone.

The Cult of the Warrior

The cult of the warrior is deeply rooted in the history and traditions of cultural and organizational leadership. Beginning around the twelfth century, the Japanese samurai devoted their lives to *bushido*, the "way of the warrior," a strict code of conduct demanding loyalty to one's master and honor to death and beyond. The European equivalent was the feudal code of chivalry, which did not go quite as far in its ethical code and practice demands. It was characterized by hyperaggressiveness, hypermasculinity, and, despite the chivalric code (or myth), a disrespect for women. In both codes, the warrior was devoted to protecting his master, the master's family and property, and the master's honor beyond his own. The code incorporated and aggrandized the use of weaponry, constant battle, and the facing of death.

One problem with the warrior legacy is it considers women as prizes or booty. The bonding relationships of men with men supercede those with women except in a sexual context. As you may well have experienced firsthand, this makes collaboration and support difficult when men and women are supposed to be working side by side as equals. Part of the dilemma for both men and women is that much of this "cult of the warrior" behavior is a shared expectation: men expect to do it, and women expect it of them.

> DO YOU BELIEVE IN THE "CULT OF THE WARRIOR"? IF YOU'VE BEEN AFFECTED BY THE WARRIOR CULT IN YOUR WORKPLACE, WHAT CHANGES DO YOU FEEL MUST BE MADE IN YOUR ORGANIZATIONAL CULTURE? WHAT CAN YOU YOURSELF DO TO BE A CHANGE AGENT? IF YOU'VE BEEN A PARTICIPANT, HOW HAS THIS WORKED FOR YOU OR HINDERED YOUR ADVANCEMENT IN YOUR CAREER? HOW HAS IT IMPACTED YOUR PERSONAL LIFE?

On Mentoring Men

I asked a group of male research participants to respond to their level of agreement with their organizational experiences. Again, as with the women, the issue of race appeared prominently in the discussions. All groups of participants were compared to Caucasian males (the reference group). There were commonalities among all males; however, some responses to questions showed differences in perceptions of organizational experiences based on race.

Males were more likely than females to agree that formulating policy is not vital to their role within the organization; that success is based on performance outcome not policy development; that they have decision-making authority within their organization; and that their organization has given them important projects to ensure their visibility and upward movement.

Asked about their level of agreement with statements relating to mentoring, competition, and receiving equal respect and appropriate attention in the workplace, men's responses differed based on race. More than likely, men of color were not mentored by Caucasian or Black women in their workplace.

Blacks (and women) were more likely to agree that their superiors considered competition among their peers as a positive activity. Black men, like Black women, did not feel that they received equal respect or appropriate attention (i.e., engaged conversation, respectful tone dialogue, responsiveness to queries, and so on) from Caucasian and non-Caucasian staff members. Black men, like Black women, men were more likely to agree with the statement, *My organization values traditional white universities in making its promotion choices.*

Caucasian men (and women) agreed that Caucasian women mentored them in their workplace; however, it was unlikely that their mentor was a woman of color, specifically a Black woman.

Caucasian men, like Caucasian women, were more likely to agree that their superiors considered competition among their peers a negative activity, that they received equal respect from all staff members, and that they experienced equal respect or appropriate attention. Caucasian men (and women) were more likely to disagree with the statement, *My organization values traditional white universities in making its promotion choices.*

> MEN, HAVE YOU EVER BEEN A MENTOR OR PROTÉGÉ IN YOUR ORGANIZATION? WHAT WAS THAT EXPERIENCE LIKE FOR YOU? IF IT NEEDED IMPROVEMENT, HOW DO YOU FEEL THAT IT COULD HAVE BEEN IMPROVED? WHAT COULD YOU HAVE DONE TO MOVE THE PROCESS FORWARD?

Question One

I asked my research participants the question: *How did you receive your position within your organization and what do you believe contributed to your being hired?* A multiple choice question, the possible answers were executive search firm, mentoring, networking, job performance, and fit within corporate culture. At 92 percent, men of color overwhelmingly said that they received their positions through job performance; other responses were networking at 84 percent, executive search firms at 25 percent, fit within corporate culture at 17 percent, and mentoring at 6 percent. Caucasian males felt that they received their position through job performance at 53 percent, networking at 26 percent, executive search firms at 13 percent, and fit within the corporate culture at zero percent. Following are sample comments from Caucasian males respondents.

- Chief financial officer, age 55

    Reading the Wall Street Journal extensively and was able to discuss it with the hiring managers and senior executives who interviewed me . . . had industry experience, track record of success, visible work ethic, business and professional references, and good chemistry with the hiring manager.

- President, age 52

    Being at the right place at the right time.

Responses from men of color were, as noted above, significantly different.

- Executive director of national conferences, age 40

    Being mentored by a senior VP of my organization, establishing a solid rapport and relationship with him, and aligning myself with him because he is the one I will report to. Experience, expertise, and education assisted me in obtaining the interview; however, ultimately my ability to be exposed to highly visible, powerful decision makers helped me receive the job offer. Receiving letters of recommendation from senior executives within the organization helped also.

- District manager, age 45

    Through work experience and performance. Having excellent references and excellent communication skills, along with the exposure to mentors who assisted me.

Men of color were more likely than Caucasian males to seek employment through executive search firms, and obtain their position based on job performance.

Question Two

Men also considered this question: *What do you believe is most important or key to your advancement within your organization?* Their multiple choices were mentoring, job performance, fit within corporate culture, and access to influential people. Men of color responded that job performance, at 37 percent, was most important; other responses were fit within the corporate culture, 21 percent; mentoring, 16 percent; and access to influential people, 11 percent. Caucasian males said that job performance was important at a rate of 60 percent, while access to influential people was 53 percent, mentoring was 40 percent, and fit within the corporate culture was just 20 percent.

Caucasian males made the following comments about advancement in the workplace.

• Executive director, age 49

> *Most important will be due to performance results—primarily with annual goals. Also key will be building relationships with key individuals within the company and working collaboratively with others. Visibility and perception of my abilities by others is also very critical.*

• Director of finance, age 45

> *Experience, expertise, knowledge, willingness to learn, enthusiasm, inquisitive nature has helped me advance. However, my ability to deal with the political climate and culture within my organization has also helped me achieve my goals, and having access to powerful people has helped me advance as well.*

Men of color agreed that performance and experience counted most toward career advancement.

• Director, age 43

> *Performance—it's what it's all about for organizations. Being a team player and having the proper attitude so that people will take note of that and remember who you are. Having access to influential people, and being mentored by someone who is in power has helped me to*

achieve greater successes.

• Sales manager, age 40

> *Show and prove when the opportunity was present. Create the opportunity when it is not present, and make yourself useful to all important, powerful senior personnel.*

All men felt that job performance was key to advancement in their careers, while Caucasian men felt that having access to influential people helped them advance more in their career than any other group.

Does Gender Matter?

I asked male and female research participants that they respond to this vignette: *You have a choice to be assigned to a mentor or protégé by the name of Ted or Rachael. They are executives who work at least two levels above you or below you. Both are well respected by senior executives, their direct reports, peers, and are highly successful. Which one would you choose?* The answers they could choose were 1) men, 2) women, 3) either gender, and 4) the person with whom I feel a connection. Men stated that they would choose men 85 percent of the time. Women, at 60 percent, said that they would choose women. Both men and women, at 15 percent, said they would choose either gender, and 40 percent of men and women said they would choose the person with whom they felt a connection. While you may feel more comfortable with your own gender and those you experience chemistry with, what is evident is that there's still a desire to have a fulfilling relationship with your mentor or protégé.

The gender of your mentor or protégé matters. Your choice of a mentor or protégé should depend mainly on what you expect to get out of the relationship, and where you want this relationship to take you in your career and personal life. As you seek a mentor and protégé, your primary goal should be one of personal growth, development, and transformation.

> TAKE A STEP BACK AND THINK ABOUT YOUR OWN EXPERIENCES. WHO WOULD YOU CHOOSE TO BE YOUR MENTOR OR PROTÉGÉ? WHAT ATTRIBUTES MAKE A GOOD MENTOR AND PROTÉGÉ? THINK ABOUT WHY YOU FEEL THIS WAY. IS YOUR WAY OF THINKING HELPFUL OR A HINDRANCE TO YOUR CAREER?

Climbing the ladder, although important, should be secondary. It's not always about where you end up, but how you get there, and appreciating the purpose of your journey.

Men Mentoring Women

Consider the advantages to having a male mentor. Research participants cited key strategies that helped them advance in their career—highly visible assignments that are also challenging, access and exposure to higher-level executives, commitment, sponsorship, and protection. Research participants (both men and women) said their male mentors offered greater assistance than their female mentors. Why? Think about your own career experiences, not only with mentors and protégés, but also with executives, managers, and supervisors—whether male or female. What are some of the experiences that you've had with your colleagues, male or female? How has your experience been with a male or female mentor or protégé?

One issue that emerged from my study was that women are much harder on women. Women are naturally communal and nurturing; however, in the workplace where power and control play roles, it may be a different story altogether. Maybe you've heard coworkers whispering behind someone's back saying things like, "She's too power hungry; I don't like being around her" or, "He's so insecure about a woman taking his job that he'll step over anyone to keep it." These thoughts may come from stereotypes, roles, and labels associated with gender in corporate America.

We've learned that workers see power differently based on their gender and race. Participants in this study believed that men had more power than women, and in different forms. Again, would you rather have a male mentor or a female one? In my research, women said men were more effective in assisting with career upward mobility. Male mentors can help women overcome those three levels of discriminating barriers we looked at in the last chapter. Men may also be better positioned to introduce women to highly visible executives, which can help advance a career. Due to the perception and reality of their power in the corporate structure, men may be able to help women get to the top rung of the corporate ladder.

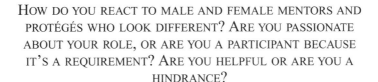

How do you react to male and female mentors and protégés who look different? Are you passionate about your role, or are you a participant because it's a requirement? Are you helpful or are you a hindrance?

In spite of this, I saw that 60 percent of women in the study would choose women as mentors. Oftentimes women are more approachable, sharing, warmer, and better at bridging the gap between the sexes in the workplace. Women are good at role modeling and counseling, offering acceptance, friendship, and personal support. Part of the issue surrounding who chooses whom as a mentor is based on the perception that women are effective negotiators. Women negotiate just as often as men, though they're more likely to engage in the negotiating process with other women because the comfort zone is high due to their similar risk of adverse societal judgment. When asking for more money, resources, or a promotion, men and women approach the request differently, not because they're innately different, but because when seeking to negotiate, women are societally punished more than men. This risk makes women more reticent. Women mentors help to build their protégé's confidence readily and bond very quickly.

There is a flipside; however. Studies show as women climb the corporate ladder they tend to behave as men by how they talk and react to other women.[1] The American Psychological Association, Journal of Applied Social Psychology, Journal of Applied Psychology, Journal of Management Development, and American Management Association offer studies that echo these sentiments. Examples include language that is defeminizing, and the adoption of a more information focused and adversarial style. This creates a culture clash (i.e., what society expects of a woman, and what is expected of persons with high level and high status positions in corporate America where male-gendered leadership traits are valued.) Often, language and styles are chosen, veering away from the side of the spectrum that is feminine. For ambitious women, language can be an injurious and potent tool when the male managerial model is negotiated. Yet a managerial style that is feminine is viewed as ineffective. Therein lies the rub. What is the solution? Women are increasingly steering away from corporate success that is defined by the male managerial model. Men, in smaller numbers, are also deciding to steer away from that model. For men and women, by embracing this behavior creates an environment of civility, increased job satisfaction, productivity, and morale. It's a work in progress, but a step toward the right direction nevertheless.

Lending a Helping Hand: Men and Women Working Together

Both practically and legally, men and women should expect equal opportunity to develop their management potential, leadership skills, and decision-making ability, and an equal opportunity to climb the corporate ladder. But there's no getting around the long history of male dominance in corporate America, or the fact that men and women are just (to use a nonscientific but accurate term) wired differently.

Responsible, visionary, success-oriented men recognize that they have to see women as full partners in the corporate world, whether in a mentoring relationship, supervisory role, or anything else. Men have to be aware that their work/life balance, attitudes, knowledge, and experience may be fundamentally different from their women peers at the office.

In some cases men and women are incompatible on the job because their personal and family perspectives are so different. A man's assumptions about a female coworker often flow from personal relationships with their daughters, wives, or other influential women. When a man is married to a stay-at-home mom, he may have a difficult time imagining a woman running an organization as he considers who to hire or promote. This also fits with the unconscious belief in some men that women don't desire to be upwardly mobile, and aren't in the workplace to stay. Also, there's an attitude that a majority of women aren't strategic in their thinking and decision making, and therefore can't possibly be good leaders. Finally, because the corporate structure is based on patriarchal command-and-control theories and behaviors, some men insist that only one leadership style exists, which is hierarchical and authoritarian.

But if men in authority will consider every worker on merit based on demonstrated ability, they may more readily commit themselves to workplace equality and whatever changes it takes to achieve that. When men are willing to speak out specifically in support of treating women appropriately, that's a key indicator that an organization is reaching a new level of commitment to women in the workplace.

Once a company has decided to reach out strongly and specifically to women, it has to make sure all the men are on board. There are four steps in particular that companies should consider in moving forward to address these issues:

1. Seek as much insight as possible into men's thinking about specific issues relating to gender in the workplace.
2. Examine the cost/benefit ratio for changing men's behavior, which is likely to strongly favor the change.
3. Place more emphasis on potential benefits of men's changed behavior.
4. Determine which processes and techniques are most effective in both initiating and sustaining new and improved behavior and attitudes toward women. The prospects for success in this area are far better when working with men if your approach addresses the relevant rational and cognitive issues.

Men should also take a highly visible role in workplace training on gender issues. This might begin with small focus groups of men and women, both together and apart. Having open and honest discussions about what you believe and what others believe helps you see your colleague's perspective, whether male or female. Talking with colleagues from different departments, and having departmental or team meetings, training, and team-building workshops helps you see where issues overlap and commonalities can be found.

Women are usually the ones who deliver training, which unfortunately helps maintain the sense that whatever is going on is about women's issues and not so much about men. Therefore, it makes a huge impact when men and women conduct workshops as partners. The list of opportunities to help goes on and on. For example, men could participate in training to help address inappropriate behavior displayed by other men. Another effective idea is to encourage interaction and informal training around social events when people are more relaxed and perhaps more inclined to consider new ideas. Man-to-man mentoring programs specifically addressing gender issues might work well.

In the end, these kinds of efforts should significantly improve conditions for men and women working side by side.

Can We Talk? Communication Styles and Gender

Who Talks Too Much?

Believe it or not, men can talk just as much or more than women, and during meetings can take up more space and time. When women are talking, they're interrupted more by men. Men tend to interrupt and "talk over" women when they're speaking, but women don't interrupt men nearly so often. Stereotypical thinking might have led you to assume just the opposite.

Body Language

Women nod their heads to indicate they're listening and paying attention, but to a man that signal usually means, "I agree." She wasn't nodding, "Yes, you're right," but rather, "Yes, I do hear and understand." On the other hand, when a woman is talking to a man and he just stands there in a neutral posture without nodding or saying anything, the woman may think he didn't understand or that maybe he's bored. More likely he is listening attentively, but doesn't indicate any specific response. A woman may become uncomfortable and ask, "Do you understand?" or constantly repeat herself, thinking she isn't being clear. Men tend to think that women who behave in this way are not confident enough, too talkative, or not assertive enough to be leaders.

Eye Contact and Approach
In order to create a connection and relationship, women use more eye contact in a conversation than men will. Men may take this behavior as a challenge to their position or power. Beginning a conversation, men tend to approach someone from a side angle while women tend to approach from the front. Men likely interpret a female colleague's face-to-face approach as too aggressive or too personal. But if a man talks to a woman in a side-to-side stance, she may interpret the behavior as deceptive or not being up-front with her.

Relationship Building
Most women love relationship building and are relationship oriented when accomplishing a task. Oftentimes women are comfortable seeking the assistance of others and know whom to approach for help with completing a task. This process builds relationships. Men tend to be more task oriented and task focused rather than relationship focused.

Because they're interested in opinions and consensus building, which also enhance relationships, women often process and think out loud when seeking a solution. The more task-focused men tend not to ruminate aloud so much about their options; they process internally to get the job done. As a result, women often think men are being unresponsive to suggestions, and men often think that women are looking for approval or don't know what they are doing. Some men think that a woman's way of processing is a sign of weakness. Not so! It's just different.

Note that these are research-based cultural norms and that not everyone fits these generalizations. Nevertheless, these characteristics and behaviors are displayed by a majority of both men and women based partially on how their brains function, resulting in different learning patterns and acculturation. In these and other ways, mistaken gender-based assumptions, which seem relatively minor, may easily ruin a good working relationship before it gets started.

How do you respond to and communicate with different genders? Are you an accident waiting to happen, or can others learn from you?

Gender Wars: Bridging the Gap

What's important to you, based on your gender, may not be important to your colleague. To move forward in your career and help others move forward in theirs, you must be able to embrace differing communication styles and build gender equity in your workplace. Understanding how men and women communicate differently, both verbally and nonverbally, can put you on the road to a more mutually fulfilling working relationship. Leverage the strengths of your male and female colleagues by breaking past biases based on both conscious and unconscious stereotypes. Men need to make room for the vital contribution of women not only because it's right, but because it will probably make your business more profitable. Women need to claim their place in the corporate world, and needn't apologize because they don't think and act the same way men do: women, you're not men.

If you're a man who processes ideas internally and you're approached by a woman asking for your opinion, feel free to let her know that you hear what she's saying, and you're processing your thoughts. Women, you may want to let a man know when you're processing your decision out loud.

SOME PEOPLE USE MENTORING AND NETWORKING INTERCHANGEABLY. WHAT IS YOUR DEFINITION OF THE TWO? HAS YOUR DEFINITION OR YOUR DEFINITION BEEN HELPFUL OR HARMFUL TO YOU OR THOSE THAT WORK WITH YOU?

This way he'll know that you're not asking him for advice on what to do. Do a bit of homework and learn more about differing communication styles, and embrace both the male and female way of doing things. Use communication style differences to achieve greater goals by finding similarities—without being afraid to recognize and acknowledge differences.

The worldwide economy is imposing diversity that, as a nation, we will be hard-pressed to match. Your company needs the brightest and best workers in the world—men and women of every race and age group—to keep up with the competition. Make sure you have the mind-set and processes in place that will enable all to be their best, so your company will be its best.

Alas, Odysseus remains a swineherd to Circe (if he retains any of his fabled luck). Hector remains a pup. Penelope weaves on forever, as her suitors swarm, while the Olympians appeal to the deposed Titans to find a "coach" for Telemachus, to teach him to bend Odysseus's mighty bow.[2]

Action Item
- Be open to differing ways of thinking, being, acting, and doing in your career and your life.

Chapter 10: Embracing the Challenge of Change

Change is not merely necessary to life, it is life.

—Alvin Toffler, American writer and futurist (b. 1928)

The world is changing faster today than ever before, and it seems like the pace will only accelerate in the years ahead. Almost every company and every job in America is being transformed by change and there's nothing anyone can do about it. But you do have a choice. You can allow change to frighten you into panic or inaction, or hide in your little corner of the office and hope nobody notices you're there. Or you can see change as a fantastic opportunity to move forward to a better job and a better life.

Our goal in this book has been to help you understand how to navigate these uncertain and choppy seas and ride out the storm regardless of who you are or how you earn a living. We hope you've been challenged to change your thinking about achieving success and fulfillment in the workplace. We've explored the five essential steps to personal fulfillment on the job, and considered effective ways to deal with roadblocks, the pitfalls of success, and other specific challenges that may come up along the way. These steps will lead you to a satisfying work context where you can succeed and still be yourself.

We've also talked a lot about specific aspects of change: in job responsibilities, your network of allies, your attitudes and assumptions toward coworkers, your own self-image and expectations, and more. At the same time these shifts and realignments are taking place, your company, your industry, and the corporate world in general is changing dramatically as well. Understanding and embracing these "macro" changes will help put the final touches on unlocking *Your Personal Power-Up*.

During the past fifteen years new competitive realities have forced corporate leaders to deploy new strategies. Shifts in international political power, the increasing strength of emerging players on the international trade scene, the transfer of commerce to the Internet, and other wide-ranging changes have encouraged fundamental shifts in the structure or corporate operations.

This emerging corporate culture is based on practices of openness, in which you as an individual are self-organizing and self-optimizing. The processes between group members are dynamic and whole with a free flow of information, rather than compartmentalized, linear, hierarchical, and constrained. This type of work environment has increased the demand for emotionally intelligent workers and emotionally savvy leaders.

Corporate leaders have learned that flattening out the traditional hierarchy allows more people to make meaningful contributions to the company's performance. Instead of a few people in corner offices calling all the shots, the organization benefits from the emotional intelligence of the whole group. Companies are also discovering a strong link between their productivity and efficiency and the degree of diversity they're committed to. The more gender, racial, and cultural diversity there is in the organization, the better it tends to perform.

Tracking the Trends

Looking at the matter in more detail, the question is whether and how each of us as individuals and organizations in general wholly engage the diverse intelligence and talent of the most gifted and educated people available, regardless of whatever demographic group they represent.

The United States population is undergoing a major demographic transformation. The non-Caucasian population in 2002 comprised 27 percent of the total. In twenty years, that percentage will rise to 38 percent; by 2050, 48 percent of U.S. citizens will be people of color. Overall, the racial and ethnic makeup of the United States has changed more rapidly since 1965 than during any other period in history—but corporate senior executive leadership has changed very little.

The interests of the United States will change as the population of less developed countries expands. Currently, the U.S. is the third most populous country on earth after China and India, yet it comprises less than 5 percent of the world's people. During the course of the next twenty-five years, world population is on track to increase by 29 percent, with nearly all growth occurring in less developed countries and with a slight shift toward becoming less male-dominant (that is, with a shift to a lower male-to-female ratio) than in 2000. These changes will have a strong and direct impact on how multinational corporations think about their markets and position themselves.

The globalization of information and technology is creating new contenders and serious challenges to the international business stronghold of the United States. IBM released an analysis showing that during 2003 more than 60 percent of new investment projects were created in international emerging markets. Almost one in three new investments in so-called back-office operations, such as call centers and transaction-processing centers, were in India. And while Western Europe and North America are still managing to attract a significant portion of direct foreign investments made by multinational corporations, they are facing strong competition from emerging markets. Other analyses confirm the challenges facing U.S. multinationals.

Indeed, some of the largest global players already embrace diversity; they draw a direct correlation between the wide-ranging talents of a diverse employee base and their ability to respond rapidly and successfully to the challenges of a world market. Corporations with women on their executive teams had significantly higher returns on equity and total return to shareholders than those without. Further, there is a strong link between an organization's productivity and efficiency and the degree to which its staff is diversely composed. For example, the Social Security Administration, which received one of the highest ratings for productivity and efficiency among federal agencies, is also among the most diverse of any federal agency in terms of employment.

From a capitalist perspective, we are at once relieved of the need to justify promoting diversity through the invoking of a national conscience or a transgenerational sense of guilt. We do, however, need to acknowledge that the playing field is still not level for all participants and that the legacy of race and sex discrimination has left its mark.

> CAN SOME GOOD EVER COME OF MULTICULTURALISM, CULTURAL COMPETENCE AND DIVERSITY IN THE WORKPLACE? IF NOT, WHAT CAN AND WILL YOU DO TO CHANGE YOUR ORGANIZATION'S CORPORATE CULTURE?

We then have to face the probability that women generally, and people of color particularly, may be unprepared to take advantage of opportunities that may be opening in corporate America. Further, corporate America may be unprepared to take advantage of a vast workforce demographic that is emerging. Communication and commitment have helped close these gaps between opportunity and preparedness, and we trust they will continue to be less of an obstacle in the future.

Most notable is that all factors over which a person might have control—such as earning post-baccalaureate degrees, performing one's job well, networking—are the very factors that seem *not* to play a role in the exclusion of women and women of color from the boardrooms and executive suites of corporate America. Having been denied both formal and informal access to influential people and organizational networks that are key to long-term success, these workers will likely need more than these tools now in order to catch up; many of them will be unable to deal with the negative self-images they've formed and the negative racial and ethnic images that still linger in the halls of power.

Judith: Keeping a Clean Conscience
Judith G., a forty-seven-year-old Asian Indian female, is a successful, knowledgeable, and creative executive director of public relations who has been with her multinational organization for five years. An M.I.T. honors graduate, Judith has lots of power and influence in her organization. Many of her colleagues come to her when they desperately need to get a job accomplished, and senior executives appreciate her high ethical standards.

However, despite her skills and accomplishments, some people see Judith as nothing more than a beautiful airhead. In fact, Byron, the executive vice president of public relations, avoids her when she tries to set a meeting with him, specifically because he knows some of his colleagues think she's a space cadet, and he doesn't want them to suspect he associates with her. With the help of a sympathetic cafeteria waitress, Judith finally "stumbles into" Byron and gets the appointment she's been wanting. After talking with her, and after realizing she has really solid and potentially lucrative ideas, Byron realizes he and his colleagues have completely misjudged Judith based on her exotic and beautiful appearance. At the core she is a brilliant and valuable member of the organization.

Byron and Judith eventually develop a trusting, productive working relationship. He admits hearing rumors about her being all looks and no brains; he knows that she openly embraces her culture and religion in the workplace, and that friends advised him to stay away from her. Byron further admits to Judith that he does not want to be an outcast among his fellow senior executives as a result of associating with her.

Not only does Byron apologize for his assumptions and change his behavior, today he is Judith's mentor. Byron introduces Judith to all of the right people, helps her to become highly visible, and she eventually receives a promotion to vice president of public relations after two years.

Judith learns not to degrade others nor place them on a pedestal, to treat everyone with respect, and never take any relationship for granted, because she'll never know what department head they will replace, or when she will need to ask for help. At the end of the day, while surviving the dance of corporate politics, Judith learns to keep her values intact by never compromising her integrity. Judith knows that to survive corporate politics she should never sell her soul to the highest bidder.

Byron learned that Judith wasn't what she seemed to be. He judged her at first by her appearance, and by how others labeled her. Once he got to know her, he realized that in spite of her gender and cultural orientation she was an important and valuable member of the organization. Judith held onto her self-confidence and improved her prospects for advancement with a new mentor, without changing her standards.

Teach Others How to See and Treat You

Picture yourself in a room surrounded with mirrors. You can see yourself in all mirrors, but you're only in one place; the perception is that you're in every place, but you're not. Everybody at work sees you from a little different angle. At the same time you look one way to one person or group, you look another way to a person or group with different assumptions and points of view.

Judith knows all about the challenges of dealing with these multiple yet simultaneous images others have of her. Here's how she explained it to a group of young MBA students:

> *If you're physically attractive, it is sometimes perceived by others that you have no depth, knowledge, or any other attribute besides the physical. Many people in corporate America can only relate to people that fit their idealistic stereotypes of what a corporate executive should look like.*
>
> *What you have to do is create a package that demonstrates who you are, what you know, how you got there, coupled with what you look like. By doing so, you will always catch people off guard and they will be pleasantly surprised. And that's when you can achieve your ultimate goal.*
>
> *Whether you are a person of beauty, a person of color, male or female, handicapped, or categorized in any other way, you cannot let anyone have power over you. It's up to you to put together what you want people to perceive. Teach people how to react to you and treat you. Never play the victim role. Contend with the hand you've been dealt and make it work for you. If you spend time thinking*

why, how, or why isn't, you won't be able to achieve your goal. Place that energy on something else.

Multiculturalism: The Kaleidoscope of Opportunity

Multiculturalism refers to people of different cultures, languages, and beliefs occupying the same territory and needing to live in a cooperative manner. Except for accents, your first reactions are often triggered by your preconceptions about another's ethnicity, gender, age, religion, or social class. Multiculturalism is based on possessing an understanding, respect, appreciation, and acceptance of differing cultures. It has become a popular term because the word *race*—as a concept—is losing its former credibility. Traditionally America prided itself on being a melting pot of diverse peoples who are connected as part of a common culture. However, depending on whom you talk to, the melting pot metaphor appears to some as oppressive assimilation. In other words, you can only be a part of the melting pot if you assimilate; otherwise you're an outsider. There are those who wish to preserve their unique and diverse cultural, racial, and ethnic communities without melting everyone into one common culture. They see America as a quilt of many distinctive colors, shapes, styles, and textures.

> DO YOU KNOW SOMEONE WHO ISN'T OPEN TO EMBRACING DIFFERENCE? DOES YOUR ORGANIZATION SIMPLY PAY LIP SERVICE TO DIVERSITY OF THOUGHTS, ATTITUDES, AND PEOPLE? DO YOU FEEL THAT EMBRACING DIFFERENCE HAS BEEN SHOVED DOWN YOUR THROAT?

We don't automatically assume that you have a desire generally to get along with people who are different from you, though we hope you do. We do assume, however, that cooperating with every type of people is best for all involved because it makes your own life easier.

Perceived and Perceiving

Taking one final look at some of the workplace changes employers and workers at every level will continue to deal with in the years ahead, I asked a group of research participants to respond to this vignette: *You are entering an organization for an interview with a hiring manager by the name of Carson Peters. What do you believe the hiring manager will see first and why?* Both men and women primarily responded that the manager would see race, race and gender, gender, or age first. However, the responses differed based on both gender and race. The participants did not know the race of the hiring manager. They only determined from the hiring manager's name, Carson Peters, that this person was a male. Here are some general results of the group response:

- Race
  Caucasian males at 1 percent and Caucasian females at 8 percent stated that the hiring manager would see race first when interviewing an applicant. Black males at 77 percent and Black females at 80 percent mirrored that sentiment, but at a significantly higher rate.

- Gender
  Caucasian males at 22 percent and females at 68 percent stated that the hiring manager would see their gender first. Black males at 2 percent and females at 4 percent mirrored that sentiment, but at a much lower rate.

- Gender and Race
  Caucasian males at 5 percent and females at 1 percent felt that the hiring manager would see both gender and race when interviewing an applicant. Black males at 21 percent and females at 13 percent agreed.

- Age
  Caucasian males at 37 percent and females at 20 percent felt that the hiring manager would see their age first. In their responses, Black males and females (at zero and 1 percent respectively) felt that age was not an important characteristic.

DO YOU KNOW SOMEONE WHO TRIES HIS BEST TO BLEND IN? HOW DO YOU SEE THAT BEHAVIOR IMPACTING HIM, YOU, AND OTHERS IN YOUR ORGANIZATION? DO YOU SEE HIM AS "SELLING HIS SOUL" OR MERELY TRYING TO SURVIVE?

Detailed comments from some of the participants shed further light on both general attitudes and how different one person's perception can be from another:

- Executive director, Caucasian male, age 49

    I've never really given the subject much thought. Perhaps those persons sitting around thinking about this may be very closed-minded. However, a person's experience is the first thing that hiring managers see.
    - Regional director, Caucasian male, age 51

    Age is the first thing that becomes obvious in these situations once you turn fifty.

- President, Caucasian male, age 55

    I am a tall white male. There is no question that this has helped me get jobs in the past.

- Director, Caucasian female, age 43

    In this day and age, how old you are will be what a person sees first, then gender, and then race. The main thing a person wants to know is if the candidate can do the job. That is the number one concern.

- Program manager, Caucasian female, age 42

    Race is the first thing that people see. It is the most obvious characteristic.

- Engineer, Caucasian female, age 47

    I believe that weight is a physical characteristic many hiring managers observe and consider.

- Director, Black female, age 48

    My skin color is my calling card. That is the first thing people see. I am judged by my skin first and everything else is secondary until people get to know me, then they see past my exterior.

- Senior vice president, Black female, age 52

    I think generalizations or suppositions as to what type of employee I might make are initially drawn from my race.

- Vice president, Black female, age 30

   The hiring manager would see my gender first, and then my race. Society is so conscious these days about gender bias and race relations, and some executives are seeking to hire certain members of their staff based on gender and race in order to be politically correct.

- Executive director, Black male, age 46

   Race is still a dominant factor in society.

- Senior systems engineer, Black male, age 42

   Race is the first thing that people see. That's human nature, and this is what we have been taught in society since the beginning of time. It cannot be hidden. It is right there in your face, and people who say they do not see race first are being dishonest with themselves, in my opinion.

- Director, Black male, age 40

   I am of the belief that people will pay closer attention to my demeanor as a Black man if the hiring manager is white. If I mirror the hiring manager, I have a better shot at being taken seriously. As for other options, the hiring manager will know that I am a male, and he will know my approximate age based on my résumé. Unless I am trying out for basketball, my height will not be an issue to him.

Don't Lose Yourself

People will make assumptions about you the minute you walk in the door. Think about what characteristics you see in others when you're simply meeting them for the first time in a business setting, or passing them on the street. Do you treat other people differently if they look different? Of course, you can't put yourself in other people's shoes literally, but you can be empathetic and sympathetic in your day-to-day dealings with them.

We'd all like to be successful in our careers and have a fair chance. But if you look different from the people at the top of your corporate power structure, you may feel a necessity to assimilate, acculturate, and compete in order to survive. In order to assimilate, your ethnic group becomes absorbed and, quite frankly, loses its distinctiveness and blends in with the majority culture.

When you acculturate, at an individual level you've come in contact with different cultures and you're culturally transformed. However, acculturation at a global level occurs as globalization develops, because of the impact of cultural contact on an international level. As you assimilate and acculturate, you're able to compete in the workplace.

Picture yourself walking into a room where no one looks like you, dresses like you, or even speaks like you. What is the first thing that comes to mind? What's the first thing that you want to do? What are some of the things that you're whispering to yourself?

Now picture yourself in your organization or a specific industry. Do you find that perhaps you rarely encounter people of your same gender, age, race, or ethnicity? How about those of you who speak English as a second language? Do you find yourself trying desperately to fit in and belong so you won't seem different from others?

If you're one of these people, you may feel that you've lost yourself in the process of simply trying to maintain your career, and oftentimes you may wonder if you've lost yourself.

In essence, it's not about your gender, ethnicity, race, or age. It's about being part of the human race. If you employ your emotional intelligence and self-efficacy skills, you will see that whether or not you have to assimilate or acculturate is not the issue. It's about knowing who you truly are and learning how to bring your true self to the workplace daily. We hope we've been able to help you see how to accomplish that.

Building the Cultural Bridge

The key to multicultural success is getting along and living in cooperation with others regardless of their heritage and background. The goal is to yield greater productivity from all involved. One of the ways to get along is to learn to respect differences for what they can contribute to productivity. Here are some questions to ask yourself and your team members: Does your workplace embrace multiculturalism and diversity? Does it require a "new you" to be accepting of differences? Do you believe it to be a lip service objective in your organization? How can you build the cultural bridge across the divide?

DOES YOUR WORKPLACE HAVE A CULTURE THAT EMBRACES MULTICULTURALISM AND DIVERSE THOUGHTS? HOW DO YOU FEEL ABOUT THE FACT THAT YOUR ORGANIZATION DOES OR DOESN'T HAVE A CULTURE CONDUCIVE TO DIVERSE PERSONS AND THOUGHTS?

Your response to workplace diversity reflects your individual ability to respect, embrace, accept, and understand the uniqueness and difference of everyone. It includes not only gender, age, race, ethnicity, religion, culture, and socioeconomic status, but also language, values, dress, sexual orientation, physical and mental abilities, political and other beliefs, family, social, and community responsibilities, among other things. It's important that you're a culturally competent individual not only in your personal life, but also in your career and organization.

Being culturally competent is about your willingness and ability to value the importance of culture as you offer and deliver services to all segments of the population. It's about your ability to respond to and value the differences of people at all levels of your organization and both your internal and external clients. Cultural competence is about being family oriented, community focused, and developmental in your way of thinking and decision making. As you move forward in your career, you can practice your cultural competence through mentoring and coaching, training and development, and teamwork that's charged with achieving local, regional, international diversity goals of your organization. Your ability to understand the importance of cultural competence in your life is critical to the successful alignment of your beliefs, values, and assumptions in your career and personal choices.

Bringing It All Together

Here's a recap of our five steps to surviving and thriving in the workplace:

Step One: Know Yourself

You can't begin to reach your full workplace potential for satisfaction and success until you peel back the various outer layers that have formed over the years and get to your authentic self.

Step Two: Resolve Contradictions

The business world tends to make assumptions about you and generally fails at understanding who you are and what you can do. Once you've discovered your authentic self, it's time to introduce everybody else to it by redefining yourself on your terms instead of theirs.

Step Three: Embrace Change; Enable Yourself and Others

Change will either swamp you, or carry you forward into the future on top of a powerful wave of opportunity and fulfillment. Rather than making a futile effort to stand against change, learn to accept change and make it work for you.

Step Four: Get Comfortable

Round up strategic allies, resolve personal conflicts with coworkers, identify political sensitivities, understand both the written and unwritten rules of your business, know when to collaborate and when to compete, enable and empower others, and sweep away the roadblocks that have prevented you from thriving on the job.

Step Five: Carpe Diem, Seize the Day

Seize the day by creating and claiming a workplace environment where you can succeed.

People the world over are in a constant state of transition between conflict and cooperation. We've offered case studies and examples to help you see where on the scale you are, and how much of the conflict you experience is from baggage that's actually yours versus how much is from your ancestors and reference groups.

Victoria's aggression produced submissive cooperation rather than collaboration and that posture was one that she wished her father had adopted in his world. Jimmy the fighting Irishman had adopted a fighter's stance toward the world and a fighter's mentality. Unfortunately a large part of that Jimmy couldn't own or live up to. Beth's empathic leadership style played well with her subordinates, but failed to operate well at upper management levels. Each of the characters you've been introduced to shows some discomfort in positioning along the conflict/cooperation continuum. These characters represent the senior executive and middle management levels in the workplace—all with leadership responsibility. Each one continues to do well essentially by remaining open to new knowledge and being willing to learn even from very junior people.

The downfall or shortfall of many of the characters is the reassertion of the negative self just in time to interfere with personal and professional advancement. You don't want this to happen to you! The presence and persistence of the negative self is the major reason for discomfort in finding an operational place between conflict and cooperation. In fact, the securing of that operational place is a function of the emergence of the successfully striving self. The purposive striving that we have suggested is the hallmark of a healthy work adaptation is leveraged most from this position and is the key to your successful interaction with others. The negative self is the natural enemy of the purposively striving self.

We have talked about self-efficacy, that blend of self-sufficiency and self-confidence that carries with it the expectation of succeeding. Self-efficacy is the key to leadership. If leadership development is the way out of many a corporate minefield, then your self-efficacy has to be developed. It works this way: self-efficacy points to leadership, leadership points to purposive striving, and purposive striving points to successes.

In the matter of Cora and Lillian we have touched upon the issue of situational ethics. Ethics is the practice or execution of principles laid down elsewhere. Those principles constitute a morality, whether laid down by religion or by humanism. Cora and Lillian's dilemma was that the situation dictated what they could do while their principles dictated that they do more. Assessing your context calls for strategic thinking. Cora's strategy was to try to solve her problem serially. It worked out for her. Lillian decided that compromising was not good for her long-term, so she moved. Many others are not so fortunate.

You read stories about many characters throughout the book. The main goal is to demonstrate that, you too, like the characters, must endure the many changes that occur not only in your career but in your personal life. You too must be able to adjust. You, too, must get to know yourself, your values, what motivates you, and whether you can affect change in your organization through developing your allies, like the stories of Jason, Carson, Francis P., Savannah, and several others have illustrated.

More and more you will experience ongoing changes in the workplace due to technological advances, increased competition, and globalization. The sooner you're able to be strategic in every aspect of your career, and acknowledge that it's becoming more and more difficult to separate your work life from your home life, the more you'll be able to endure. This book offers you many weapons to place in your arsenal that will help you move forward in a sustained manner in both your career and personal life. Down the road you may find yourself asking which way you should go just as Alice in Wonderland did; however, this time, you'll have the answer because you'll know who you are (your authentic self), what is important to you (morals and values), and what you want to get out of life and offer to others (*purposive striving*).

Throughout our book we have illustrated how you can be comfortable in your own skin. You won't develop self-awareness overnight, and it may take a lifetime to fully realize your true self. We've looked at characters who, although fictitious, face real-world personal and professional problems, centering on respect and the quest to receive appropriate attention—whether from superiors and coworkers or family and friends. The consequence of this is enduring difficulty in finding a place in the cooperation-conflict continuum from which to leverage your efforts in the world. The research discussed here reveals that it's a continual challenge for corporate professionals to be seen and valued for who they are and for what they can do.

We want to challenge business professionals to be fully aware of your true selves. Cooperation and collaboration will have to trump competition and conflict, though they will never entirely replace them. The goal is to help you be empowered, fully committed, and effective, armed as you are with unique important and personal gifts. The findings here will also enable business professionals to provide new opportunities for yourselves, your organization, and your leaders. The challenge to becoming comfortable in your own skin is not chiefly about relationships between people, but between individuals and the corporate identity.

A Satisfying Sense of Success

Against all odds, against the trends, against expectations, you have the power to transform your workplace experience. You can move from a place of self-doubt and fear of change—symbolized by what we call the negative self—toward recognized and identified goals: purposive striving. You can move from a workplace characterized by conflict to one of cooperation. This doesn't mean there won't be setbacks and frustrations along the way. Certainly there will be. Life won't be completely without stress, but it can be manageable, satisfying, and with a sense you are in control rather than blown around by the whirlwind of self-serving and myopic corporate and organizational policy.

You will have the confidence to cope with whatever comes along. And if it's not possible to reach your goal where you are right now, you'll be able to recognize that and make a change just as confidently as if you were making decisions about what to do if you stayed put.

You will feel a satisfying sense of success. Being more confident and relaxed, you may well do your job better and enjoy it more no matter what the circumstances. And if you make more money, too, that's fine as well. The purpose of these steps is not primarily to raise your salary, but if it makes you a more confident and content employee, it's likely to make you a more productive one in the process.

You don't have to live your life and spend your career trying desperately to pretend you're somebody you aren't and making yourself miserable. You have the power to be true to who you really are deep down, the power to have a the power to have a satisfying and fulfilling career without selling out, without abandoning your personal goals and standards, without compromising the person you are at the core. You have the power to take control of your life, move resolutely toward achieving the goals you set for yourself, and enjoy the satisfaction, relief, and peace mind that comes from a job well done.

You have the power. Like little Dorothy in *The Wizard of Oz*, you've had it all along. Now use it.

Action Item
- Begin your journey to becoming fully you.

End Notes

Foreword

1 "Gallup study: Feeling Good Matters in the Workplace," *Gallup Management Journal*, 12 August, 2009. Gallup.com, gmj.gallup.com/content/20770/Gallup-Study-Feeling-Good-Matters-in-the.aspx (accessed 17 October, 2009).

Introduction

1 "APA Poll Finds Economic Stress Taking a Toll," *American Psychological Association*, 7 May 2009. APA Online, www.apa.org/releases/stressproblem.html (accessed 10 December 2009).

2 "2007 Electronic Monitoring & Surveillance Survey," Reuters.com 28 February 2008, www.reuters.com/article/pressRelease/idUS179098+28-Feb-2008+BW20080228 (accessed 17 October 2008).

3 "Mayors Release New Metro Economies Report at 2nd National Summit on Energy and the Environment," Press Release, 26 October 2006, U.S. Conference of Mayors, www.usmayors.org/metroeconomies/1006/metroeconrelease_102606.pdf (accessed 17 October 2008).

4 "2007 Catalyst Census Finds Women Gained Ground as Board Committee Chairs," IMDiversity.org, 10 December 2007, www.imdiversity.com/villages/woman/business_finance/catalyst_boards_2007_1207.asp (accessed 17 October 2008).

5 "Statistical Overview of Women and Diversity in the Workplace," Catalyst Information Center, www. Catalyst.org.publication/132/us-women-in-business (accessed 15 January 2009).

6 "Oldest Baby Boomers Turn 60," Facts for Features, 3 January 2006, U.S. Census Bureau, www.census.gov/Press-Release/www/releases/archives/facts_for_features_special_editions/006105.html (accessed 17 October 2008).

7 "Gallup Study: Feeling Good Matters in the Workplace," *Gallup Management Journal*, 12 January 2006, Gallup.com, gmj.gallup.com/content/20770/Gallup-Study-Feeling-Good-Matters-in-the.aspx (accessed 17 October, 2008).

Chapter 2

1 Excerpt from Kurt Cobain's suicide letter, widely available on the Internet.

Chapter 4

1 Thinkexit.com Quotations, Albert Bandura Canadian Psychologist, http://thinkexist.com/quotation/we_find_that_peoples_beliefs_about_their/154847.html (accessed 11 June 2009.

2 About.com: Women's History Marie Curie Quotes Marie Curie (1897-1956) By Jone Johnson Lewis, About.com http://womenshistory.about.com/od/quotes/a/marie_curie.htm,(accessed 15 September 2009).

3 Mia Hamm quotes (American female Soccer Player. b.1972) Thinkexit.com Quotations http://thinkexist.com/quotation/no-one_gets_an_iron-clad_guarantee_of_success/151368.html, (accessed 8 June 2009).

Chapter 7

1 "Invictus" by William Hensley (1849-1903) widely available on the Internet.

Chapter 9

1 "Internalized Mysogyny and the Politics of Gender in Corporate America," *Journal of Psychoanalytic Social Work*, May, 2009, Volume

16, 1-11.

[2] Fellows, B., & Thomas, C., *International Journal of Mental Health*, "Changing Roles: Corporate Mentoring of Black Women. A Review with Implications for Practitioners of Mental Health", Winter 2004-05, Vol 33, 4, p.14.

Acknowledgements

The authors wish to acknowledge the assistance of the following individuals in the preparation of this book: Leadership Excellence; Cedric W. Fellows, M.B.A.; Katherine Gaskins; David Goggin, M.B.A. and Julie Goggin, J.D.; Brian G. Smith, M.A.; the model of the late Pearl Thomas; the Union Institute & University (TUI) Research Committee: Wise E. Allen, Ph.D., Douglas V. Davidson, Ph.D., Leland K. Hall, Sr., Ph.D., Alice H. Thomas, Ph.D., Claudewell S. Thomas, M.D., M.PH., B. Lynn Ware, Ph.D., and Lloyd C. Williams, Ph.D.; and Literary Agent, Eric Valentine.

About the Authors

Brenda McGlowan-Fellows, Ph.D.

Brenda Fellows is an industrial/organizational psychologist, professor, author, speaker, and corporate consultant providing management consultation to leaders in major private global corporations, the public and non-profit sectors. She is a graduate, with distinction, from The Union Institute and University of Cincinnati, Ohio. Dr. Fellows' 2003 dissertation research, *The differential perception of the ability to be hired and promoted in the workplace based on race and gender*, is considered seminal in her field of study.

Dr. Fellows is President and CEO of Fellows Corporate Consortium, LLC, a San Francisco–based global management consulting firm specializing in corporate consultation in the fields of industrial/organizational psychology, social psychology, organizational development, organizational behavior, behavioral management, human resource management, mental health administration, sociology, clinical counseling, and curriculum and instruction.

Dr. Fellows has spent her twenty-year professional career in sales and marketing management, training and development, finance and administration, operations management, regional and district employee management, and business development within Fortune 50, 100, and 500 corporations. Her areas of expertise include industrial/organizational psychology, social psychology, organizational development, organizational behavior, behavioral management, and human resource management.

Dr. Fellows' award-winning research centers on creating effective containers for all persons to work and grow together. She has found that building capacity in people and systems allows organizations and their leaders to add enormous value to the outcomes critical to their success. Recently her work has focused on helping women move beyond the "glass" and "concrete" ceilings in corporations through the use of mentoring, emotional intelligence, executive coaching and strategic leadership development.

She is a recipient of the Circle of Scholars Award for Outstanding Academic Achievement and Seminal Dissertation Research in a Field of Study, was nominated for the Marvin B. Sussman Award for Outstanding Academic Achievement and Seminal Dissertation Research in a Field of Study, and is a recipient of the Avice M. Saint Graduate Management Award for Outstanding Scholastic Achievement and Leadership in the Field of Management.

Currently, Dr. Fellows is an Adjunct Professor in the Haas School of Business at UC Berkeley. She is a Thesis Advisor and has provided instruction to graduate and executive learners in the MBA and MIB programs of Grenoble Graduate School of Business in Grenoble, France, and the London School of Business and Finance in London, England. Dr. Fellows has also provided instruction to graduate and executive learners in the MBA and Doctoral Programs of the Swiss Management Center University in Zurich, Switzerland, Santa Clara University's Leavey School of Business, and the business schools of Notre Dame de Namur University, San Jose State University, and San Francisco State University. Dr. Fellows is a featured speaker in U21 Global University's Management Webinar Series in Singapore for graduate, executive learners and alumni.

Claudewell S. Thomas, M.D., M.PH.

Claudewell S. Thomas, M.D., M.PH., is Professor Emeritus of Psychiatry and Biobehavioral Sciences, David Geffen School of Medicine UCLA. He has more than forty years of teaching and administrative experience at Yale, the National Institute of Mental Health (NIMH), New Jersey Medical School, the Los Angeles County of Mental Health, and UCLA. He is a distinguished Life Fellow of the American Psychiatric Association and an emeritus member of the American College of Psychiatrists and honorary member of the American Psychoanalytic Association. Dr. Thomas is a former Tavistock organizational consultant in association with the AK Rice Institute and the Washington School of Psychiatry. He is a 1997 recipient of Yale's Department of Psychiatry Distinguished Psychiatric Alumnus Award, and has been listed in as many as seven marquee editions of Who's Who simultaneously. He is an emeritus member of the scientific research society Sigma Xi and a former member of the National Research Council's (of the National Academy of Science) Assembly of Behavioral and Social Sciences. Dr. Thomas is Fellow of the New York Academy of Medicine, Fellow of the New York Academy of Sciences, and Fellow of the American Public Health Association.